I0624703

making GREETING CARDS *with* CREATIVE MATERIALS

making GREETING CARDS *with* CREATIVE MATERIALS

✳ MaryJo McGraw

NORTH
LIGHT
BOOKS

www.artistnetwork.com

ABOUT THE AUTHOR

MaryJo McGraw is a nationally known rubber stamp artist and author whose work has been featured in leading rubber stamp-enthusiast publications. Innovative techniques and creative teaching methods have made her a much sought after instructor at conventions, retreats, cruises and stores for over 15 years.

Making Greeting Cards with Creative Materials. Copyright © 2001 by MaryJo McGraw. Manufactured in China. All rights reserved. The patterns and drawings in this book are for the personal use of the crafter. By permission of the author and publisher, they may be either hand-traced or photocopied to make single copies, but under no circumstances may they be resold or republished. It is permissible for the purchaser to paint the designs contained herein and sell them at fairs, bazaars and craft shows. No other part of this book may be reproduced in any form or by any electronic or mechanical means including information storage and retrieval systems without permission in writing from the publisher, except by a reviewer, who may quote brief passages in a review. Published by North Light Books, an imprint of F&W Publications, Inc., 1507 Dana Avenue, Cincinnati, Ohio, 45207. (800) 289-0963. First edition.

05   04   03   02   01   5   4   3   2   1

Library of Congress Cataloging-in-Publication Data

McGraw, MaryJo.
   Making greeting cards with creative materials / by MaryJo McGraw.
    p. cm.
   Includes index.
   ISBN 1-58180-126-2 (alk. paper)
   1. Greeting cards. I. Title.

TT872 .M3424 2001
745.594'1--dc21

2001044315

Editor: Jane Friedman
Designer: Andrea Short
Production Artist: Lisa Holstein
Production Coordinator: Mark Griffin
Photographer: Christine Polomsky

acknowledgments

Again, I would like to thank all my friends, coworkers, store
owners and stamp company owners who have been so generous
with their time, talent and products throughout the years.

❋ Thanks to my family for all their love and support.

❋ Special thanks to the crew at North Light. It is a joy
working with such a talented crew of people, especially
Jane Friedman, Tricia Waddell, Christine Polomsky,
Sally Finnegan and Greg Albert.

❋ Thanks to Irma Deane wherever you
are! Your help and support back in the early
days was and is humbly appreciated.

table
of contents

INTRODUCTION

So many ideas, so little time. With the abundance of new materials and products to use on your greeting cards, how can anyone find time to experiment with them all? Expanding upon the traditional greeting card format, I will be using some everyday materials in new and different ways—items that might be familiar from other craft projects, such as fabric bond, decorative threads and yarns, plastic and foil wrap, shipping tags, office supply items, facial tissue, newsprint, paper towels and handmade papers from around the world. The more unusual items such as mica tiles, ROXS, copper sheeting, watch crystals and picture pebbles, although more difficult to find, give your personal greeting a unique look.

TOOLS *and* MATERIALS

❋ RUBBER STAMPS

There are generally three parts to a rubber stamp: the mount, the cushion and the die. Quality mounts are made from hardwood. The cushion is made of foam from ⅛" to ¼" (3mm to 6mm) thick. The die, the most important part of the stamp because it transfers the design, should be closely trimmed. In some projects, I use metal stamps, which are available at most hardware and some stamp stores. They are simple to use with most metals, especially thin copper.

❋ PAPER

I could write a whole book on paper! There are so many exciting papers available I can't even begin to explain the different types. So I will give a very basic way to decide what you need for a project. The thicker the paper or cardstock (card), the more adhesive you need to adhere it! Most heavy porous papers may need extra time for a glue or adhesive to sink in and set up. The more textured the paper, the more you must work it in to the surface. Most of the papers and cardstocks I have used in the book are not extremely textured, so I can use fabric bond or double-sided tape effectively.

❋ CHIPBOARD

Chipboard is a cheap, useful material (used to make cereal boxes and the backs of paper tablets). I use it in this book for a variety of card additions, such as the heart in the Dye Card. You can substitute mat board or any recycled cardboard for chipboard.

❋ INKS

There are three basic ink types: dye, pigment and solvent. Dye-based pads are the type you see lying around the house or office. Dye-based ink is water soluble. Pigment inks are now widely available through stamp and gift stores and are a good choice when using uncoated papers. They are also used for embossing and for archival applications, such as scrapbooking. Solvent-based inks are used mainly for stamping on unusual surfaces such as wood, plastic and ceramic. I use them for a nice, crisp, black outline that won't smear like dye inks do.

❋ DYE REINKERS

Dye reinkers are the small bottles of ink you normally use to refill your dye-based ink pads. Be careful when using inks straight from the bottle; they are very concentrated and will easily stain clothing. Be sure to use the smallest amount possible; you can always add more. You can also use dye ink to alter the color of water-based paints or PearlEx powdered pigments mixed with binder.

❋ DOUBLE-SIDED TAPES

Double-sided tapes come in a variety of forms. When working with most paper projects I prefer paper-lined doublestick tape, although when the surface is sheer or clear (vellum or acetate) a clear tape would be preferred. Most art supply and stamp stores carry a variety of both.

❋ DIAMOND GLAZE

I often use this dimensional adhesive because it dries to a clear, glasslike finish and securely holds many mediums. You can also brush it on thin for a laminated look. It can be used as a medium to mix with many other paint products.

❋ ACCESSORIES

Accessories such as threads, beads, paper cord, tassels, gift tags, charms and buttons can be found at most stamp stores. I also find these items in specialty stores for beads and needlecrafts. Office supply stores are great for unusual items too.

❋ BEADS

I use many types of beads and beadlike accessories in this book. The glass beads I use are tiny and have no holes. They also have a metallic finish. I also use ROXS, which is a cross between glitter and beads and makes for an eye-catching embellishment. ROXS can be embedded under Diamond Glaze or layered between embossings.

❋ PICTURE PEBBLES

Some projects use picture pebbles, which are glass marbles with one flat surface. They come in a wide variety of sizes and colors and are available in many stamp or craft stores. When placed over an image, it magnifies the design, which is perfect for small photos. When using colored pebbles, keep the colors on the image light. The clear ones are perfect for darker pieces. The pebbles are also great for quick jewelry projects.

❋ WATCH CRYSTALS

These discs can be used to enliven your artwork in a variety of ways. The crystals I have used in this book are plastic and inexpensive. I like them for a clear dimensional look. The crystals can also be filled with beads, seeds, sand, small toys and pictures. You can find these in paper specialty and stamp stores. For glass crystals and other watch parts check out the online auction sites.

❊ Bone Folder

The bone folder is a great tool for scoring paper and smoothing down creases. Bookbinders use it for turning corners and scoring. Some are made from bone, while others are made from resin or wood. They come in several lengths and are very helpful in several crafts.

❊ Craft Knives

A craft knife is an invaluable tool when creating greeting cards. The blade should be pointed and very sharp. Change your blades often to ensure clean cuts.

❊ Punches and Cutters

Many projects use a variety of paper punches, including circle punches, square punches, spiral punches and leaf punches. These are widely available at craft stores. You might consider investing in a circle cutter, which can be adjusted to cut circles in a range of diameters. In this book I also use ¼", ⅛" and ¹⁄₁₆" (6mm, 3mm, and 2mm) hole punches. Sometimes an awl will work just as well as a hole punch.

❊ Heat Gun

Look for a heat gun that is specially made for stamping: They are usually geared at a safe temperature for paper projects. Keep your heat gun away from your cutting mat, as it can distort the surface. (It's hard to cut on a warped mat.) When holding the heat gun be sure to keep your hand off of the vents. You can burn it out by covering the vents.

❊ PearlEx Powdered Pigments

PearlEx powdered pigments are raw pigments used for a variety of purposes, including making your own paints. You can also use PearlEx as a surface coating on paper or collage projects. Powdered pigments do need what is known as a "binder" to keep them adhered to your project. In this book we will be using Diamond Glaze as a binder. Other options include white glue, paint mediums, gum arabic or spray fixative. Mixing any of these with PearlEx will create a colored medium you can apply to surfaces as you wish.

❊ Tassels and Cords

Tassels make a great addition to a beautiful card. The ones used in this book are available at most stamp stores. Paper cord is also available. As you will see in this book, paper cord is an extremely versatile decorative item. Both tassels and cords are usually sold in assortments of colors.

❊ Templates

Plastic and brass templates are a great investment. They last forever, are inexpensive, and there are many types available. Look for envelope, box and card templates at stamp stores.

EMBOSSING POWDERS

To use embossing powder, stamp an image with pigment or embossing ink. Sprinkle the powder over the wet ink and shake off the excess. Use a heat gun to melt the powder and create a raised design. Be sure to have a variety of colors; embossing looks great in almost any color. Embossing powder comes in solid-color and multicolor forms.

ACETATE

The acetate used in this book can be found in stamp stores. You want to be sure to get embossable acetate (also known as "window plastic") in case you want to heat the piece. The same is true of heavy cold laminate used here; it should be embossable. The thicker the laminate is, the better for the projects in this book because of the beating the pieces will take.

MICA TILES

Mica tiles are compressed layers of mica that can be cut and layered. I use them in many projects as a decorative and protective covering over photos. They are heat-resistant, acid-free and lightweight.

METAL ACCESSORIES

Some projects include copper wire, thin copper sheets or fun metal shapes as embellishments. These items can be found at craft, stamp and hardware stores.

EYELETS

In this book I have several projects with eyelets. Eyelets are similar to grommets but are a single unit. Using the setting tool will roll down the backside of the eyelet. This tool and many colored eyelets are available at stamp and paper stores.

GESSO

Gesso is a wonderful primer paint that can be used in many projects. In this book I have used it as a primer and as a mixing agent with dyes and paints. It is the best primer I know for canvas, Styrofoam and especially papier maché. It comes in black and white and can be found at most good art supply stores.

FABRIC BOND

Found at fabric stores by the yard, fabric bond is an excellent way to adhere fibrous materials together, especially handmade papers.

VELLUM

What is commonly called "vellum" is really translucent vellum. It's a sheer paper that can be found in all stamp, paper and scrapbooking stores and is a perfect paper for overlay work. Many types come with designs already printed on one side. Its color can be altered with dye ink.

PAINT PENS

There are many types of paint pens. Many simply use the same type of paint you can apply with a brush in pen form and work effectively only on paper. For all nonporous surfaces (clays, plastics, wood, papier maché, chipboard and metal), you will need a permanent type. The only pens that I find hold true metallic color on most surfaces are the Krylon Gold, Silver and Copper Leafing pens.

COLD LAMINATE

Some laminates need heat setting to make them adhere, but cold laminate is an extremely clear, heavy acetate that is sticky on one side. This makes it much easier to use and no other equipment is necessary to get it to work. It gives any paper surface a high-gloss finish, and it can also be embossed.

ACRYLIC INKS

These inks can usually be found near calligraphy or airbrush supplies. Pearlescent Liquid Acrylic inks are very thin, making them perfect for washes and drip applications. Most can be mixed with a variety of mediums, including Diamond Glaze, gesso and many kinds of paint.

chapter one

These faux handmade papers can be made with any house-

hold paper—such as paper towels, kitchen parchment, facial tissue or

newsprint—and yet look like lovely handmade papers. You can use

these papers to decorate paper boxes, ceramic, glass or wood items.

faux paper

DYED PAPER

This is probably the easiest method I know to create a great looking paper. All you need are some paper towels and dye, and you're ready to go! The two card projects that follow this technique will put your efforts to good use—you'll wrap the dyed paper over pieces of chipboard that will create lovely accents for any card.

WHAT YOU'LL NEED

two-ply paper towels • several colors of dye ink • metallic ink or paint • small cups or bowls • water

ONE: Dyed papers begin with two-ply paper towels. Prepare several bowls of dye or stain.

TWO: Add five drops of dye or ink to two tablespoons (30ml) of water. The dye should appear darker in the bowl than the desired color.

TIP

If you would like a more metallic cast to your papers, add a few drops of acrylic metallic inks (the type calligraphers use).

THREE: Fold the towel down to a small square, then dip the corners into the different-colored dyes. Fan folding the towel will give you a different pattern.

FOUR: Once the colors have bled together, allow the piece to dry completely.

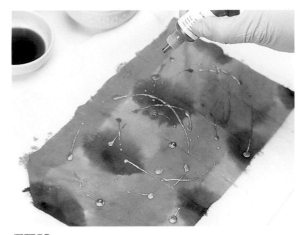

FIVE: Sprinkle metallic ink or paint over the paper surface for a splatter effect. Create several different-colored sheets using this technique. Let the paper dry overnight.

 **TIP**

If you have a very light-colored piece, stamp it with a large background stamp.

DYE
card

Once you've created a nice dyed paper from the previous technique,

experiment with this simple yet elegant card.

WHAT YOU'LL NEED

•••

dyed paper *(from basic technique demo)*

clear glue • doublestick tape • tall cardstock

chipboard *(cardboard)* • threads or fiber

rubber stamp • ink pad

•••

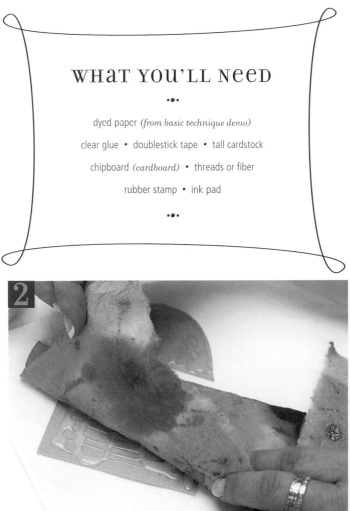

ONE: Cut a 3" x 2" (8cm x 5cm) piece of chipboard and a smaller piece in the shape of a heart. Cover the pieces of board with a coat of clear glue.

TWO: Quickly apply the dyed paper to the board, allowing the paper to retain any creases or wrinkles. Repeat the steps on the heart-shaped part.

THREE: Tear away the excess paper.

FOUR: Stamp a few images on it.

FIVE: Crisscross yarn or thread over the heart. Tie the thread together on the back side of the heart and secure with doublestick tape.

SIX: Apply a dab of glue to the board, then layer the heart on board.

SEVEN: Add doublestick tape to the back of the square and apply to cardstock.

TIP

Try colored wire strung with beads instead of thread.

paper
& bead card

This card adds a few elegant touches to the first basic card. Cut a

1½" x 3" (4cm x 8cm) rectangle and 1½" (4cm) square piece of

chipboard to start.

WHAT YOU'LL NEED

•••

dyed paper *(from basic technique demo)* • cardstock

¼" (6mm) hole punch or awl • doublestick tape

craft knife • eyelet • eyelet tool

small hammer • metallic thread • clear glue

chipboard *(cardboard)* • beads

•••

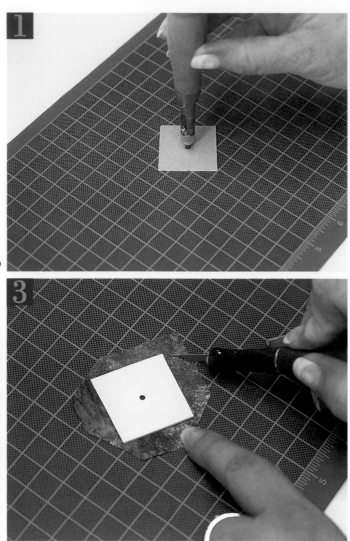

TIP

The punch I used here is a Japanese screw punch, generally a bookbinding tool. You can use a regular ¼" (6mm) hole punch or even an awl.

one: Punch a hole in the center of a 1½" (4cm) square piece of chipboard using a ¼" (6mm) hole punch.

TWO: Layer the dyed paper over the square chipboard using clear glue. Do the same for the 1½" x 3 " (4cm x 8cm) piece of chipboard.

THREE: On both pieces, trim the excess leaving about ½" (1cm) remaining. Trim the corners at an angle, leaving just an ⅛" (3mm) edge at each corner.

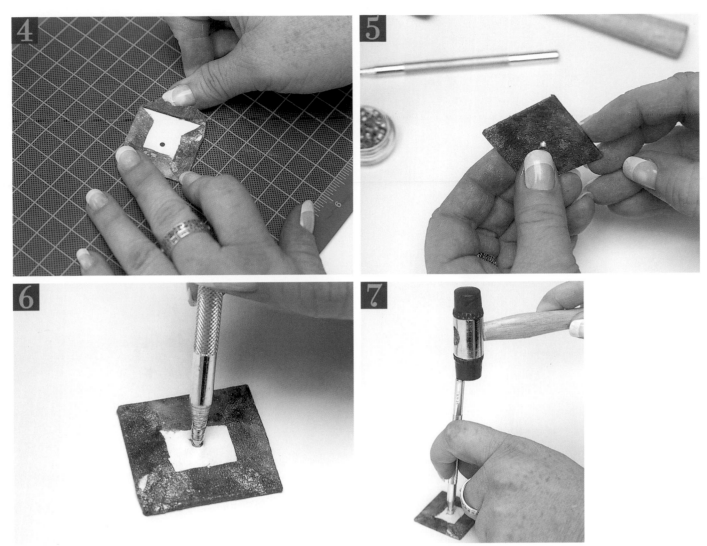

FOUR: Fold in the sides of both pieces; on the square piece, poke through the hole with an awl or needle.

FIVE: Insert a colored eyelet.

SIX: Insert the eyelet setting tool.

seven: Using a small hammer, set the eyelet on the back.

eight: Lightly tap the back of the eyelet to finish. *(Try using an eyelet in a contrasting color.)*

nine: Thread each bead on a loop of thread.

TIP

These small eyelets do not need much pressure to roll under—

just a few light taps with a small hammer!

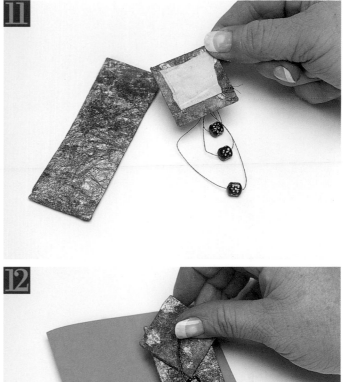

TEN: Draw the loops through the eyelet.

ELEVEN: Attach a square of double-stick tape to the back of the piece.

TWELVE: Layer all the parts onto the cardstock with the doublestick tape.

chapter two

Use napkins, paper towels, newsprint or tissues on kitchen foil to

create a very moldable paper. With this approach, you can create

some interesting shapes to give your greeting a sculptural quality.

Since the paper can be wrinkled and remolded several times, it's

great for wrapping cardboard, boxes and more. When layered back to

back, the same technique can be used to create small bowls or boxes.

sculpture paper

sculpture paper

Any scrap paper, thin junk mail, newspaper, newsprint, paper towel, napkins, bath tissue, wrapping tissue or bond paper can be used. Start with a 12" (30cm) length of heavy foil. In this case for the paper I am using a plain paper towel.

For this particular technique, gesso is used, which can be found at most good art supply stores. Gesso is a wonderful primer because it covers many items completely with only one coat.

WHAT YOU'LL NEED

kitchen foil • white gesso • paper towel • foam brush

any art medium—watercolor, acrylics or inks *(I'm using Diamond Glaze and PearlEx)*

black acrylic paint • hair dryer

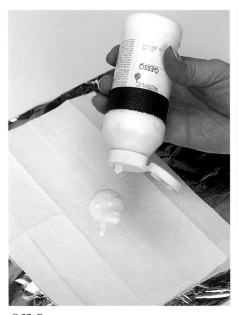

TWO: Using a foam brush, spread the gesso out. Moving any liquid paint, gesso or medium is always more effective if spread from the center of the project paper.

One: Place the paper towel in the center of the foil. Pour a 1"-wide dollop (3cm) of white gesso in the center of the paper towel.

THREE: Go over the edges of the towel. Let it dry.

FOUR: To this base paper you can apply almost any art medium including acrylic paints, inks and watercolor paints. I am using a combination of Diamond Glaze and PearlEx. The ratio of PearlEx to Diamond Glaze can vary. I usually start at four parts Diamond Glaze to one part PearlEx, then gradually add more powder for a more opaque paint.

FIVE: Apply the first color thoroughly over the gesso. Let it dry.

SIX: Crumple the base paper then lay it out flat. Using a foam brush, mix a teaspoon (5ml) of Diamond Glaze with ¼ teaspoon (1ml) of black acrylic paint. Brush this mixture lightly over the cracks of the paper.

SEVEN: To speed the drying time, try a hair dryer. Do not use a heat gun for this process—it could make the paint bubble!

copper
BUTTON *card*

After completing the sculpture paper, try wrapping it over a piece of

chipboard for this button card. The style of the button really makes

the look of this card.

WHAT YOU'LL NEED

•••

sculpture paper *(from basic technique demo)*

chipboard *(cardboard)* • craft knife • shank button

scissors • gold leafing pen • black cardstock

ROXS • tassel • hole punch • glue

doublestick tape • paper towel

•••

one: Once the sculpture paper is completely dry, trim it to the desired size.

TWO: For this card I am using a small piece of chipboard about 3" x 1" (8cm x 3cm). Wrap this board with the sculpture paper. No glue necessary!

THREE: Punch a hole large enough for the shank of a button to fit through.

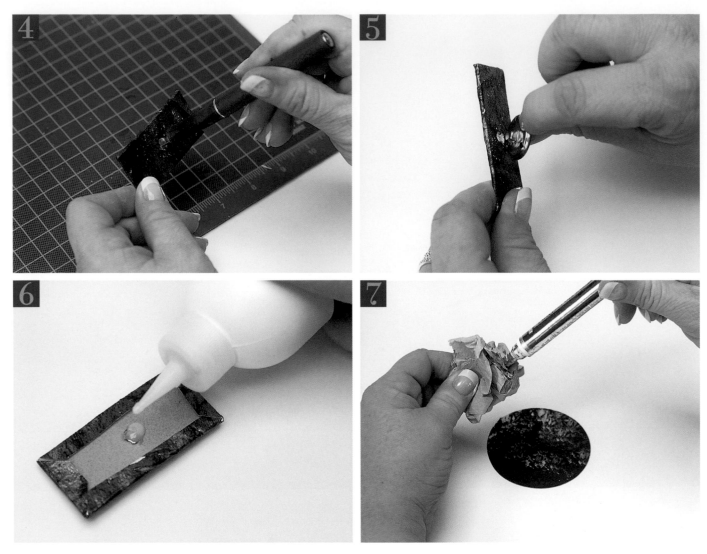

FOUR: You might need to enlarge the hole to a more oval shape depending on the size of the shank. This is easy to do by twisting a craft knife through the existing hole.

FIVE: Insert the button. It should be a snug fit.

SIX: Apply a small amount of glue to the back of the button. Set this piece aside to dry.

SEVEN: From black cardstock, cut out a 3" (8cm) circle. Apply gold leafing pen to a crumpled paper towel then stamp on the cardstock.

eIGHT: Repeat the process until the circle has been covered evenly.

nIne: Add doublestick tape to the back of the sculpture piece, then adhere to the circle.

Ten: Apply a bead of glue to the front seam.

eLeven: Shake ROXS over the glue. Allow the ROXS to set for one minute before removing the excess.

TWELVE: Once the piece has dried, adhere to a card with doublestick tape.

THIRTEEN: For a finishing touch, wrap a tassel around the button.

PHOTO
nugget *card*

Here's a variation on the sculpture paper using black gesso. This project

also uses picture pebbles, which are glass marbles with one flat surface.

When placed over an image, it magnifies the design, which is perfect for

small photos.

WHAT YOU'LL NEED

...

PearlEx • black gesso • foam brushes

paper table napkin • circle and square punches

scissors • craft knife • Diamond Glaze

acrylic metallic inks • picture pebble • color-copied photo

transparent ruler • black dye ink • rubber stamp

white cardstock plus assorted-color cardstock

hair dryer • foil • doublestick tape • glue

...

HOW TO PREPARE THE SCULPTURE PAPER

*Begin by tearing off a 10" x 10" (25cm x 25cm) piece of
foil, then lay your choice of paper on it. Plain newsprint
gives a smooth appearance, paper towels a more fuzzy
texture. For this piece I have chosen a plain paper table
napkin which tends to look like canvas when finished.*

*Pour a 1" (3cm) dollop of black gesso in the center of
the unfolded napkin and, with a foam brush, spread it
out to the edges onto the excess foil. Allow this to dry
thoroughly. (In some climates, this may be overnight.)
The gesso that seeps though the table napkin will adhere
the foil to the paper. Crumple the piece for added texture.*

ONE: Mix Diamond Glaze with a small
amount of PearlEx or acrylic metallic ink.

TWO: Brush over the wrinkles with a
foam brush. On this paper I painted half
green and the other half gold. Now I can
get the contrasting colors I need in one
piece of paper.

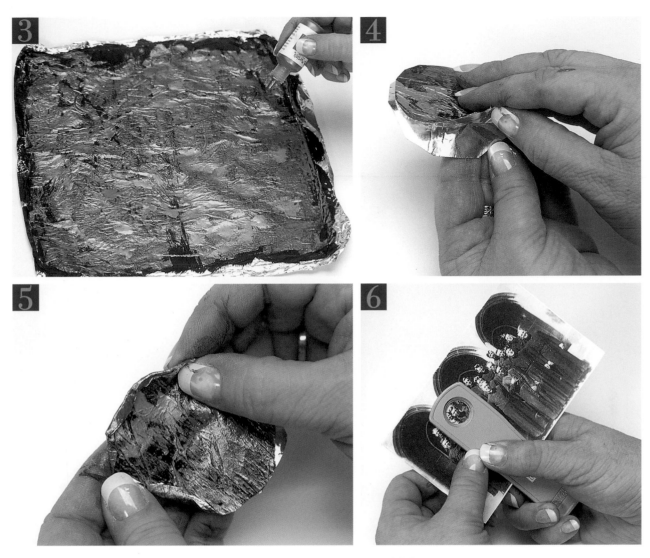

⟨⟨⟨ TIP ⟩⟩⟩

Try rubber stamping the surface with acrylic inks for a more definite pattern. Some acrylic inks now come in pads, which makes them easier to apply to a stamp.

THREE: Drizzle on inks or paints for more interest. Dry with the hair dryer to speed things up.

FOUR: Choose two contrasting pieces of the sculpture paper. Cut a circle out of each color about 1½" (4cm) in diameter. Place them together foil to foil.

FIVE: Begin rolling the edges together so that the lighter-color paper is on the inside. Mold the paper to form a small bowl.

SIX: Use a ½" (1cm) circle punch to cut a circle from a copy of an old photo.

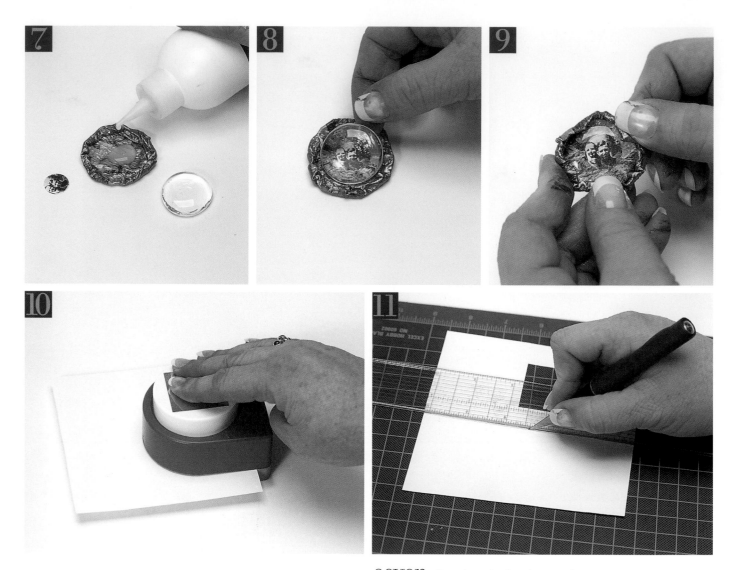

seven: Pour into the bowl a pea-size dollop of Diamond Glaze. Place the photo in the bowl.

eight: Lay a picture pebble into the bowl.

nine: Crimp the edges of the paper around the pebble. Allow the piece to dry.

ten: Punch out a 1½" (4cm) square on white cardstock. Ideally you want a ¾" (2cm) edge.

eleven: Use a transparent ruler to cut off excess from the other side.

(⌒ **TIP** ⌒)

This pebble in the bowl makes an interesting magnet. Simply glue a magnet to the back.

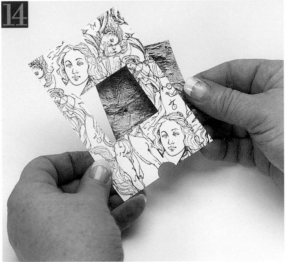

(((•••))) TIP (((•••)))

*Using just a portion of a decorative punch along the edge of
cardstock is a great way to add excitement to layers, envelopes
or pockets.*

TWELVE: To accent the two edges,
use the same circle punch used on the
photo to cut a half-circle embellishment.

THIRTEEN: Using black dye ink,
stamp several images or one large background stamp onto the cardstock.

FOURTEEN: Add a small piece of
sculpture paper behind the cutout.

FIFTEEN: Assemble card with doublestick tape; glue on the picture pebble.

| chapter three |

Duo papers are great for many projects including journals, portfolios, origami boxes and of course greeting cards—especially trifolds and accordion folds. Any project that shows two sides of a single paper is perfect. The dyed papers you created in Chapter One are perfect for the next projects because they are extremely porous and provide a perfect base for a plastic liner to adhere.

duo
paper

DUO Paper

Plastic wrap laminating is certainly not a new technique. Quite often I run into people who have made plenty of this type of paper but have never used it! Duo papers can be tricky in putting cards together because of the different-colored sides. One card that uses this paper to its full advantage is the triptych card. First let's look at one of the basic laminating methods.

WHAT YOU'LL NEED

plastic wrap • iron • lightweight handmade papers

one: Take two very distinct lightweight papers. Good choices are inexpensive tissue papers, lightweight handmade papers or any uncoated text-weight papers. Lay the plastic wrap to the back side of the first paper. Layer the second paper (good side up) over the plastic wrap.

TWO: Using a warm iron, press the two pieces together. This may require a few test runs because irons and wrap will vary.

THree: My preference is to fold the paper in half as soon as possible. This makes the crease very crisp.

⟨⟨⟨ TIP ⟩⟩⟩

The less expensive the wrap is the better it seems to work. Also, if the papers you choose are very thin, you can layer smaller die-cut paper pieces in between the two layers.

natural
LEATHER *card*

Bags of scrap leather are available at most craft stores. Most bags have a

good variety of colors and sizes that are perfect for stamping.

WHaT YOU'LL NeeD

•◦•

duo paper *(from basic demo technique)*

scissors • leather • Asian stamp or photo

assorted fibers • picture pebble • clear glue

•◦•

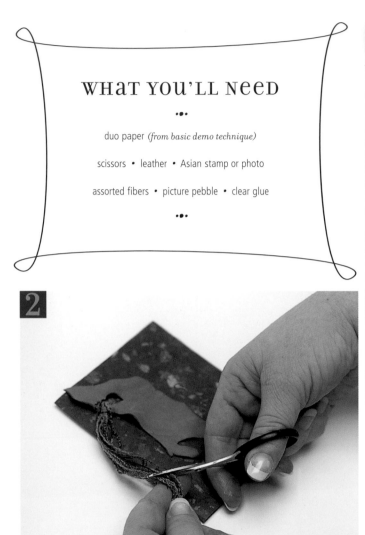

ONE: I've chosen a piece of leather with a small hole in it— the perfect size for a picture pebble to fit in snugly. Fibers and yarns will give a unique look to your greeting. Here I have attached a selection of them through the hole in the leather.

TWO: To check composition, lay the leather on the duo paper then trim the fibers.

THREE: Select a stamped image or small photo to go under the pebble. In this case I have chosen a small Asian image simply stamped in black ink.

FOUR: Once the image has dried, apply a small amount of clear glue then lay the pebble over the image. Allow this to dry thoroughly.

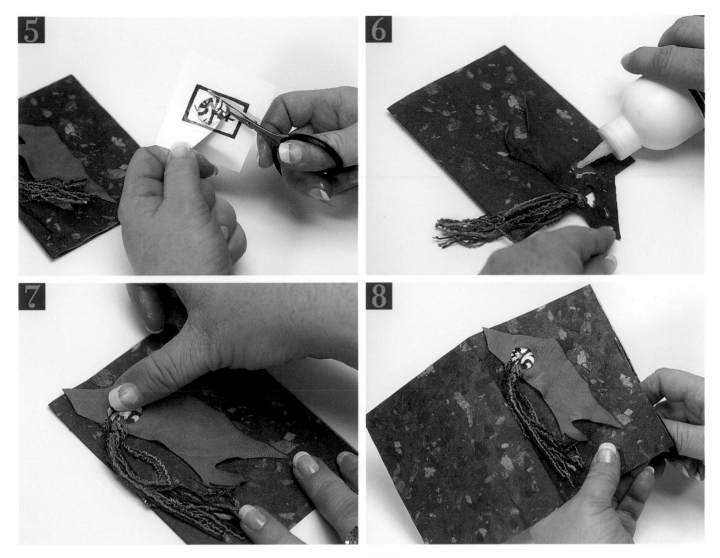

(((∞ TIP ∞)))

Leather can be stamped with black permanent ink, Colorbox

Crafter's ink or Ancient Page inks.

FIVE: Trim tightly around the pebble with scissors.

SIX: Add a small amount of clear glue to the back of the leather. Layer onto the duo paper card.

SEVEN: Adhere the picture pebble with a drop of the clear glue. Apply pressure for a minute.

EIGHT: Trim off ¼" (6mm) of the front of the card to reveal the lighter paper on the inside.

TRIPTYCH
card

This style of card can be made into an arch form or an easy double door

style. For this duo paper project, heavier papers should be used to accom-

modate the weight of decorations. Keep this in mind when creating your

duo papers.

WHAT YOU'LL NEED

•••

cardstock • heavyweight handmade paper

rubber stamps • circle cutter • PearlEx

Diamond Glaze • plastic wrap • glass pieces

craft knife • round paper clips • metallic thread

assorted beads and charms • permanent black ink

iron • doublestick tape • template on page 124

•••

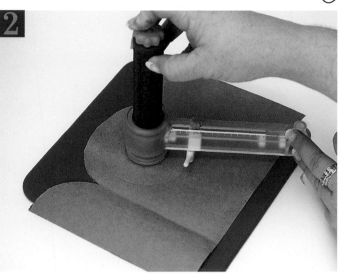

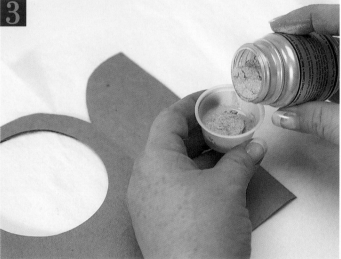

HOW TO PREPARE THE DUO PAPER

Trace the template on page 124 onto cardstock and cut out. Score the panels. Place a sheet of plastic wrap between the cutout triptych and your choice of handmade paper. Trim away as much of the plastic wrap as possible. Continue on to step one.

ONE: Press your triptych shape with a warm iron (silk setting). Trim away the excess plastic and paper.

TWO: Using a circle cutter, remove a circle about 3½" (9cm) from the center panel.

THREE: Mix about ½ teaspoon (2ml) of PearlEx with a tablespoon (15ml) of Diamond Glaze.

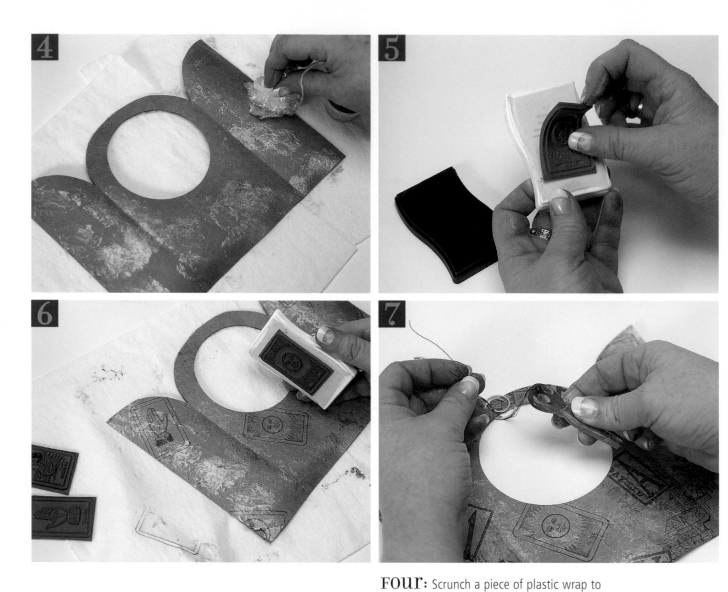

(ᗡᗡᗡ TIP ᗡᗡᗡ)

Decorating the cardstock after it has been trimmed allows more

precise placement of the images.

(ᗡᗡᗡ TIP ᗡᗡᗡ)

You can find round or wooden paper clips at specialty office

supply stores and bookstores.

FOUR: Scrunch a piece of plastic wrap to use as a texture tool. Dip into the paint mixture and apply to the cardstock. Let it dry.

FIVE: Many rubber stamp companies sell unmounted rubber only. Quite often I don't have time to mount them on wood, so I use a piece of doublestick tape to temporarily mount the rubber to a stamp pad or small tin.

SIX: Stamp and decorate the plain cardstock.

SEVEN: Bring on the embellishments! Here I have used a round paper clip to hang a large stone bead with metallic thread.

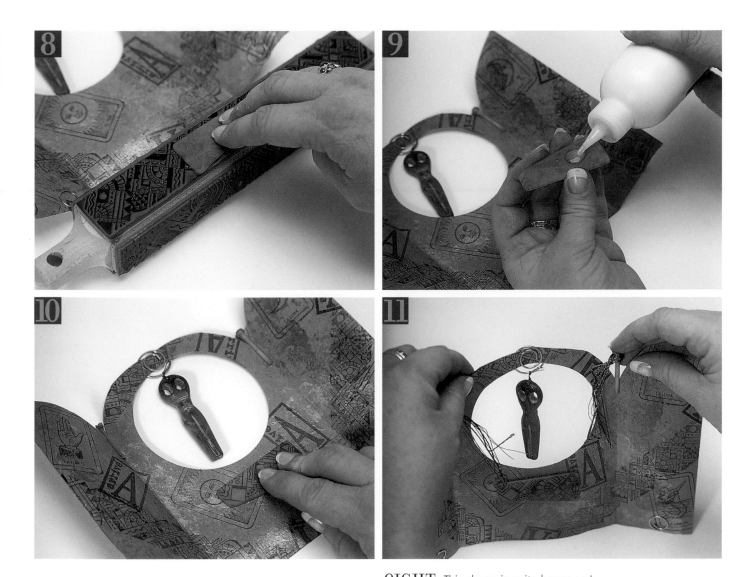

TIP

These triptychs are large cards. You can always create a smaller pattern to fit standard envelopes, but when mailing, remember to check postal requirements for added weight, depth, height and width.

EIGHT: This charm is quite heavy, so I need an embellishment of equal weight to counterbalance the card when it is standing. Here I have used a small piece of stained glass that has been sanded to give soft edges and an opaque finish. Any glass can be stamped with permanent black ink. To stamp an image on the glass, it is easier to lay the glass onto the stamp.

NINE: A small amount of Diamond Glaze added to the back of the glass will keep it adhered to the paper.

TEN: Press firmly for a minute or weigh the piece down with a heavy book.

ELEVEN: Once the glue has set, finish off the embellishments by adding wooden paper clips tied with threads or fibers.

chapter four

Use fabric bond to artfully adhere fabric, beads or ROXS and

handmade papers to cards. It will add an unusual dimensional look

to a greeting. Since thick handmade papers can be difficult to layer

together with plastic wrap because of the bumpy quality of the fibers,

fabric bond easily solves the problem.

Fabric
Bond

GOLD Leaf
circle card

This project introduces you to the interesting modern-art effect you can

achieve when using fabric bonding material.

WHaT YOU'LL NeeD

•••

gold leaf • charms or beads • metallic thread

clear laminating sheet • embossing powders

assorted-color cardstock • doublestick tape

heat gun • ROXS • fabric bond • stippling brush

•••

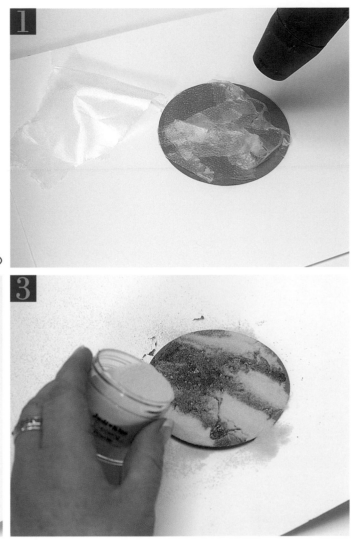

ONE: Take a few small pieces of the fabric bond. Several small leftover pieces will work. Arrange the fabric bond on a circle of cardstock or art board. Melt the material with a heat gun.

TWO: Lightly sprinkle embossing powder over the entire surface. Or, instead of embossing powder, try extra fine glitter or an assortment of tiny beads on the fabric bond.

THRee: Layer a few more pieces of the fabric bond then add another color of powder. Heat.

FOUr: While the piece is warm, lay gold leaf over the edge area. Press firmly. Allow the piece to cool then remove the excess leaf.

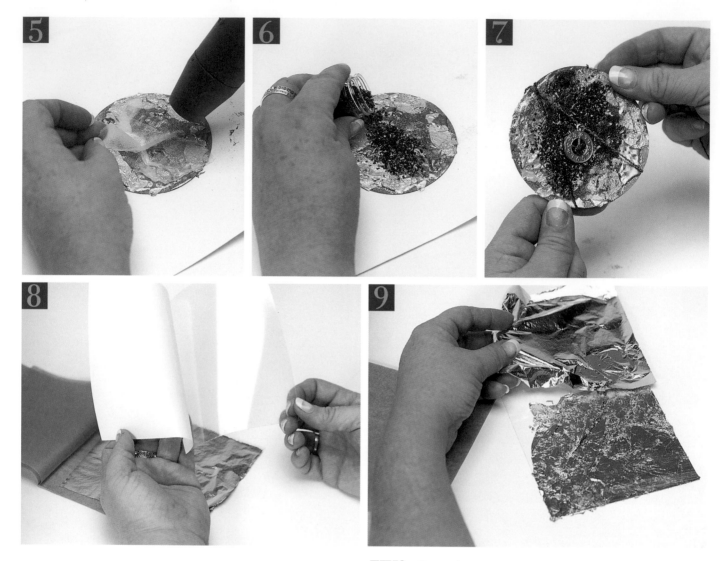

(((TIP (((

*String beads and charms before tying the thread to the card
and use a piece of tape on the end instead of a bulky knot. It is
easier to pull them into exact position while wrapping.*

FIVE: Place a few more small pieces of the bonding material on the center of the circle. Heat until melted.

SIX: Pour on ROXS.

seven: Place a charm and/or beads on metallic thread. Wrap the thread around the piece and secure with doublestick tape.

eIGHT: Create the background layer with laminating sheets and gold leaf. Peel the backing from a clear laminating sheet.

nine: Lay the sheet sticky side up. Carefully lay the sheet of gold leaf on the laminate.

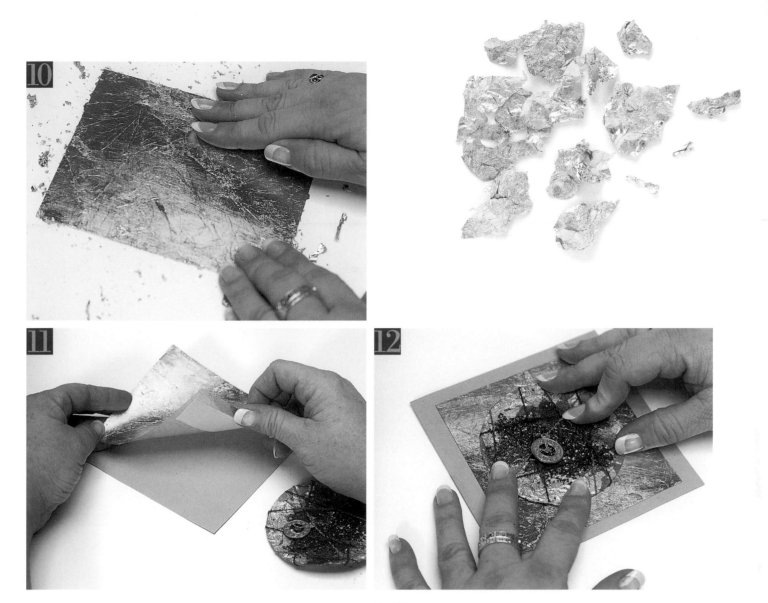

TEN: When using sheets of foil, your fingers can gently brush away the excess. Some foil comes in small pieces contained in a box or bag. For this type of foil it is best to use a stencil or stippling brush to gently brush away the excess.

ELEVEN: This technique of applying the foil to the laminate is much easier than using foil glues. Also you can use either side of the foiled laminate. If you like a matte gold finish, use the piece foil side up; if you like the surface to be extremely shiny, use the laminate side up. Either side can be placed on your card with doublestick tape.

TWELVE: Layer all the elements onto cardstock with doublestick tape.

(((TIP)))

Using a box lid or plastic tray will catch the excess foil, which you can use again. Even the tiniest piece can be used on another project. Also do not worry if the foil folds over itself, since the excess can be retrieved by softly brushing the surface.

cHinese
cHarm *card*

Introducing interesting fabric scraps and charms to your cards can add

an elegant look for a variety of occasions.

WHAT YOU'LL NEED

•••

cardstock • velvet • satin or silk fabric • charm

metallic thread • rubber stamp • scissors

fabric bond • doublestick tape

•••

ONE: Begin with a small rectangle of good velvet. About 3" x 6" (8cm x 15cm) of rayon or acetate works best. Set your iron to the wool or cotton setting. Choose a stamp with a thick-lined pattern to it. Many people use only bold stamps. Even though this stamp is small, the line is heavy.

TWO: Flip the stamp and velvet over so that the back side of the fabric is facing you. Mist the back of the velvet lightly; iron directly on the stamp for 10–15 seconds.

THREE: Choose another piece of fabric. I'm using a piece I picked up at a fabric show. I am only using a 2" x 3" (5cm x 8cm) piece. Iron the bonding material to the fabric following the package directions.

(((⌐ TIP ⌐)))

Choosing the second piece of fabric is what really makes the card. You can use a very small piece of heavy patterned silk, satin or even a remnant of upholstery material. For most heavy fabrics on cards, Leave the fabric with a raw edge. Velvet is the exception because it frays.

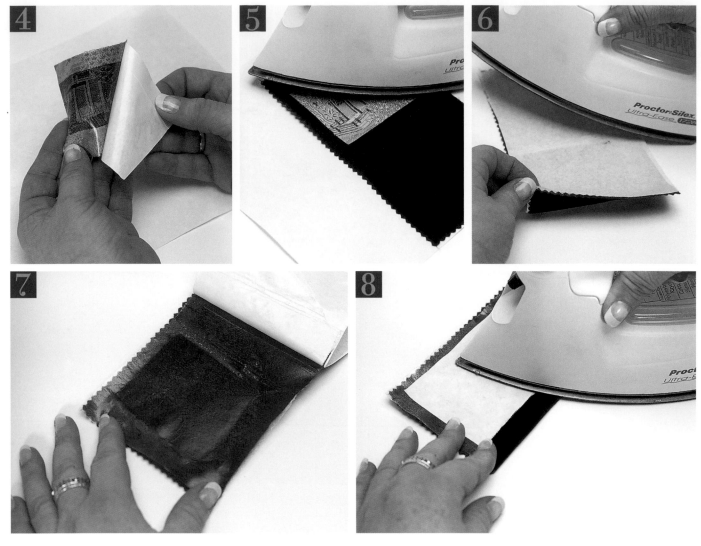

To eliminate bulky corners, trim the excess from the corners before folding in, as we did with the papers in Chapter 1.

TIP

To eliminate bulky corners, trim the excess from the corners

before folding in, as we did with the papers in Chapter 1.

FOUR: Remove the backing from the bonding material.

FIVE: Position this fabric on the front of your velvet. Carefully iron it to the velvet using the tip of the iron.

SIX: Iron the bonding material to the back of the velvet. Do not overheat or you could lose the image pressed into the velvet.

SEVEN: Remove the backing then place on a piece of cardstock cut to the desired size. In this case, it is about 5" x 3" (13cm x 8cm).

EIGHT: Fold over the raw edge. Iron down.

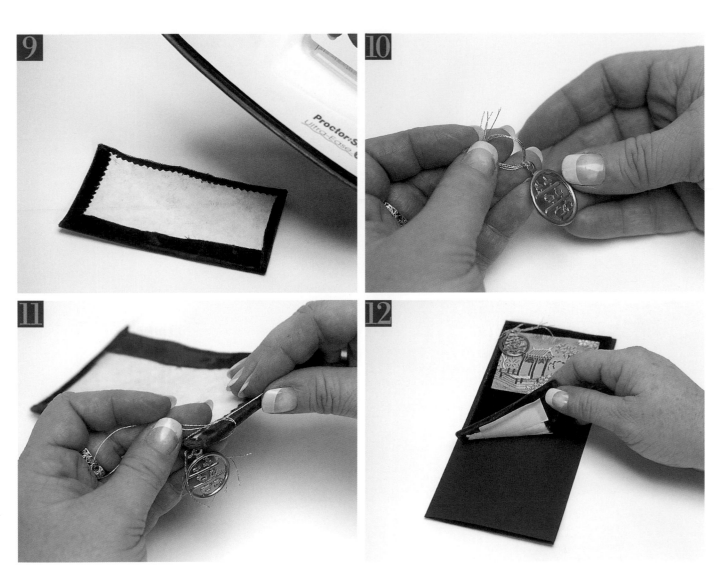

(()) TIP (())

Some fabric scraps may be very uneven. Trimming them (as I have here) in an asymmetrical shape can add interest. You may want to make a raw edge more intriguing by pulling a few threads to create a ragged look.

nine: Press the completed piece once more, especially at the corners.

ten: Create a loop with metallic thread and tie on the brass charm.

eleven: Attach the charm to the top left corner.

twelve: Add doublestick tape to the back of the piece and layer onto cardstock.

chapter five

I have taught window illusion cards for many years, and it is still

one of my favorite classes. This technique uses two layers of vellum

or acetate to create the illusion of floating elements. The second card

is an updated version of the original card using mica tiles.

m1 amour

WINDOW ILLUSIONS

BeaTnIK *card*

Select two pieces of cardstock of the same size and color. Square cards

are great for this project since the measurements will be the same all

the way around the card. This project will use removable tape, which

is available at stamp stores and office supply stores. If you cannot find

removable tape, here is a trick

that works in a pinch.

WHAT YOU'LL NEED

•••

circle cutter • two identical cards • assorted fibers

removable tape or doublestick tape

transparent ruler • paper scraps • spiral punches

stamps • acetate • craft knife • chenille yarn

•••

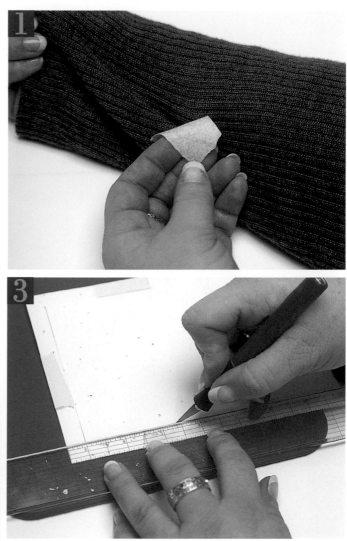

one: Take any kind of tape—here I am using the same doublestick tape I use for most projects—and place it several times on any fabric. This will create a surface on the tape that is not as sticky and presto—removable tape!

TWO: Begin by taping the two identical cards back to front.

THREE: Using your craft knife and a transparent ruler, cut a ½" (1cm) frame out of the taped section. You will be cutting through two pieces of cardstock, so be sure to have a fresh blade in the knife.

⟨⟨⟨ TIP ⟩⟩⟩

With any type of tape try not to stretch it taut, as it will pull

back to its original size causing a bubble in the tape and paper.

FOUR: Now the frame will match up perfectly when you put the finished card together.

FIVE: Apply clear doublestick tape around one of the frames.

SIX: Cut two pieces of acetate (about 5" [13cm] square and 4¾" [12cm] square) to use inside the frame. The smaller piece creates a pocket of acetate so that you will not need as much tape. Place the larger piece of acetate on the frame that has been taped.

seven: Stamp two identical images. Using doublestick tape, adhere the images back-to-back. Lay these images and other elements on the acetate.

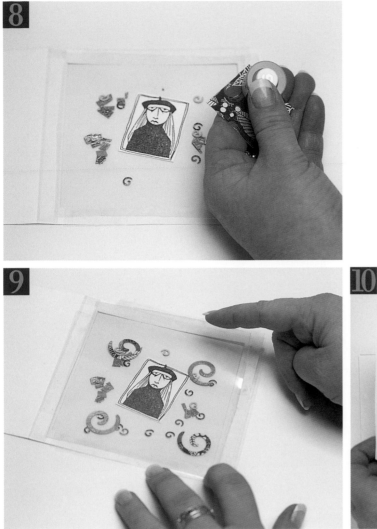

TIP

For the inside of the acetate pocket, you can also use confetti, tiny beads, colored mica chips, glitter and back-to-back stickers.

eight: Here I have used punches to create my own confetti from leftover paper scraps. Make sure the paper you are punching looks good on both sides, and try to keep all of the materials in the center of the acetate as they tend to gravitate toward the exposed tape.

nine: Sandwich your smaller piece of acetate over the tape; there should be a small strip of tape still exposed.

ten: Line up the inside edges of the second frame, then lay the top frame onto the tape.

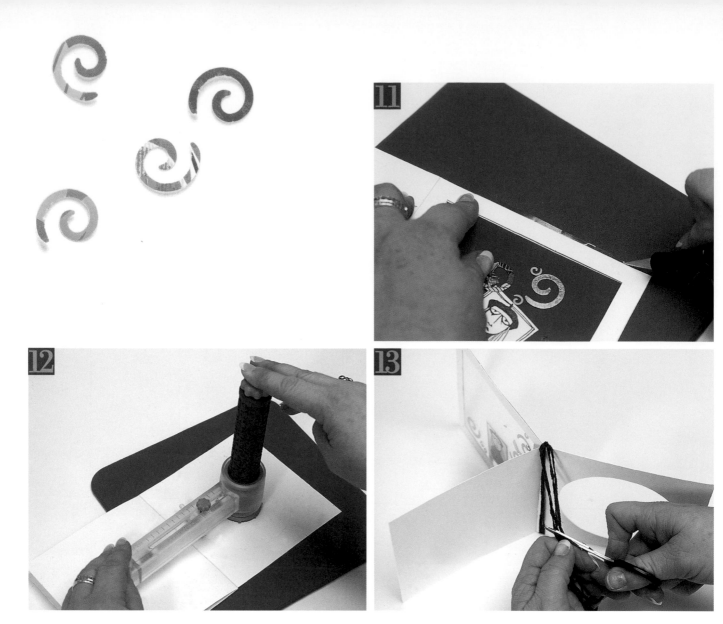

eLeven: Trim any excess tape, acetate or cardstock from the outside edges of the card with a craft knife.

TWeLve: On the front panel of the card (which can be left solid) I have created a large circle frame with my cutter.

THIrTeen: To add a bit of color, tie on a bit of chenille yarn.

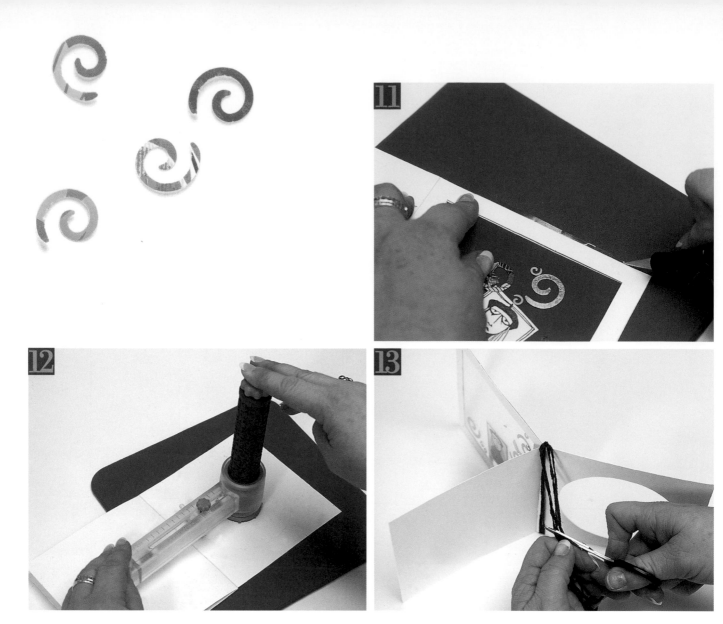

(((⊙ TIP ⊙)))

Keeping white cardstock clean is tough. Keep a white rubber eraser and craft knife nearby for quick cleanups. Lightly scrape smudges with the knife, then even out the paper surface with the eraser.

mica
HEIRLOOM *card*

I like the natural look of these mica tiles, particularly with old photos.

The crinkled texture of the mica is much more interesting than simple

acetate, especially when creating a graphically simple card. Begin with

two square cards and one dark green standard note card.

WHAT YOU'LL NEED
•◦•

mica tiles • small metal alphabet • circle cutter

two color-copied photos • doublestick tape • craft knife

thin sheet of copper • small brads • clear glue

⅛" (3mm) hole punch • two square cards • dark green

card • scissors • small hammer • black ink

•◦•

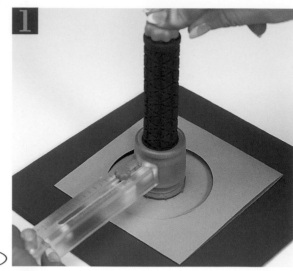

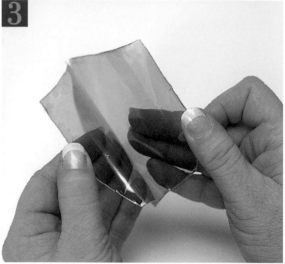

ONE: Using a circle cutter, punch or craft knife, cut a 3" (8cm) circle out of the center of a square card.

TWO: This circle should go through both sides of the card.

THREE: Carefully separate a mica tile into two thin pieces of equal size larger than the circle.

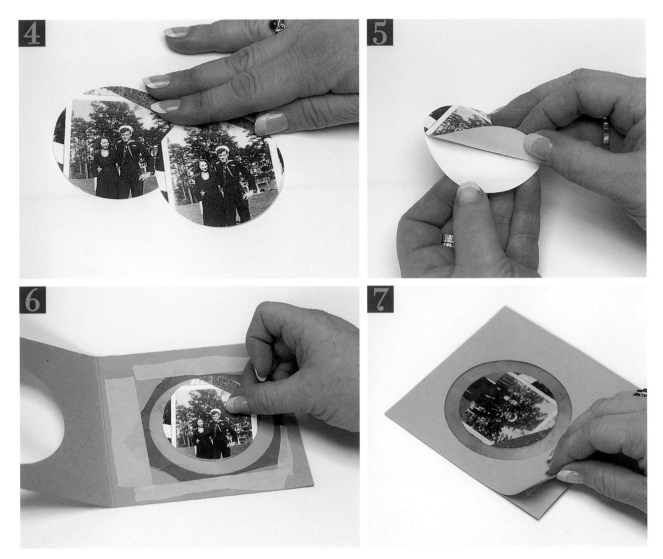

TIP

Color copy old black-and-white photos on the full-color setting to achieve the sepia-rich tones that heirloom photos have.

TIP

Mica tiles can be difficult to separate. Begin with a thick piece, then separate it in half and in half again until you achieve the desired thickness.

FOUR: Cut two smaller circles (about 2" [5cm]) out of identical color copies of an heirloom photo.

FIVE: Attach the photos back-to-back with a small piece of doublestick tape.

SIX: Insert the photos between the mica tiles. Apply a drop of clear glue to an inconspicuous spot on the photo to keep the photo in place. Attach the entire element to the inside of the card using doublestick tape.

SEVEN: Seal the card up.

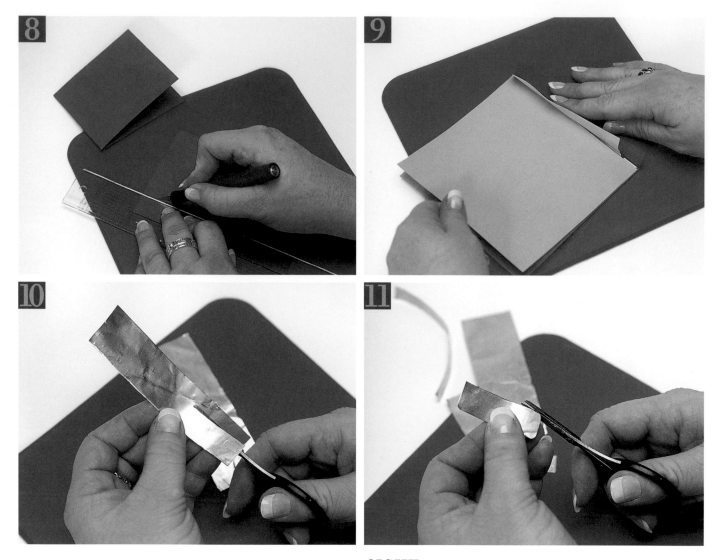

(()) TIP (())

On some of the other samples, I have simply used two cards of different colors then trimmed the front of one card to achieve the ¾" (2cm) border fold.

eIGHT: From the folded dark green note card, trim a ¾" (2cm) width of the scored fold.

nine: Cut your second square card in half; you will use one of these halves to create the heirloom card's back panel. Place a section of doublestick tape on the inside of the dark green fold. Position the fold onto the framed photo and the back panel. Press well.

Ten: Metal alphabet stamps are available at most hardware and some stamp stores. They are simple to use with most metals, especially this thin copper. With scissors, cut out a small strip of copper.

eLeven: Round off the corners.

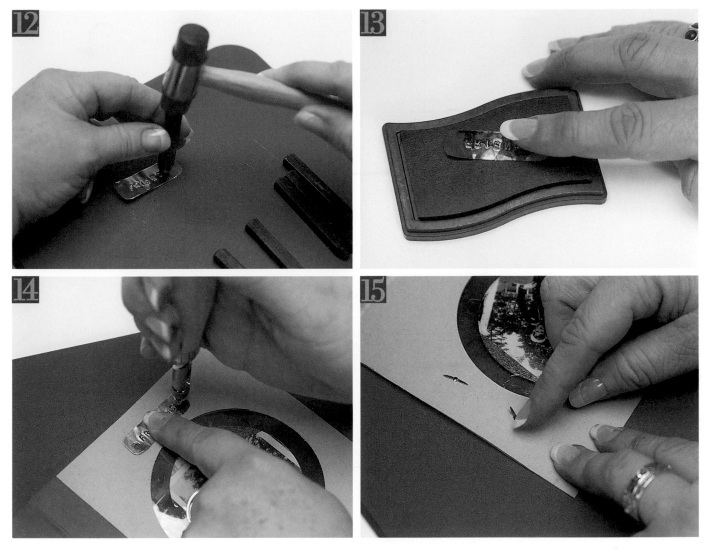

TIP

When stamping a word with an alphabet set, write out the word on a piece of paper the same size as the area to be stamped, then set the paper above the area. Begin with the center letter and work your way out to each side.

TWELVE: Holding each metal stamp straight up on the copper strip, tap the top of the stamp several times with a small hammer.

THIRTEEN: After completing the stamping rub a bit of black ink over the stamped letters; wipe any excess off of the copper.

FOURTEEN: Punch a hole on either end of the copper strip with a ⅛" (3mm) hole punch. Lay the strip on the front of the card for placement. Mark the holes with a pencil, then punch corresponding holes in the cardstock.

FIFTEEN: Use tiny brads to hold the strip in place.

chapter six

Give a new look to your greeting cards by using shipping tags.

Tags are available at discount, hardware, craft, stamp and office sup-

ply stores and come in a variety of papers as well as metal. In both

projects punches are used to add pattern and depth.

SHIPPING Tags

Leaf
Tag *card*

Gold leaf and cold laminate are generally found at craft and stamp

stores. Quite often gold leaf can be messy and

difficult to use since it tends to fly away. Cold

laminate can make the process much quick-

er and neater than glues.

WHAT YOU'LL NEED
•••

assorted leaf punches • large shipping tag

Krylon gold leafing pen • silk ribbon • tall cardstock

gold leaf • brown pigment ink • cold laminate

stiff brush • tissue • piece of paper

craft knife or scissors • doublestick tape or glue

•••

TIP

Turning a punch upside down will make positioning shapes much easier.

one: Start with a large shipping tag. Remove the string. Punch out most of the surface of the tag with a variety of leaf craft punches. These punches are widely available from craft, stamp and scrapbooking stores.

TWO: Once you have completed the punching, apply a piece of laminating sheet to the back of the tag. Trim away the excess laminate.

THREE: Lay gold leaf on the sticky side of the tag.

(ꝏ TIP ꝏ)

Pigment ink works well for this project since the paper on most

tags is uncoated. It also wipes off the foil effortlessly.

(ꝏ TIP ꝏ)

Simple geometric punches and vivid colors work well on a

birthday card.

FOUR: Press the gold leaf well into the crevices. Gently use a stiff brush to remove the excess foil.

FIVE: Color the tag with a brown pigment ink pad. The coverage on the tags is better if you apply the ink after every image has been punched; it covers the cut edges of each image.

SIX: Remove the excess ink from the gold leaf with a tissue.

SEVEN: Cover the brown reinforcement and edge the tag with a gold leafing pen.

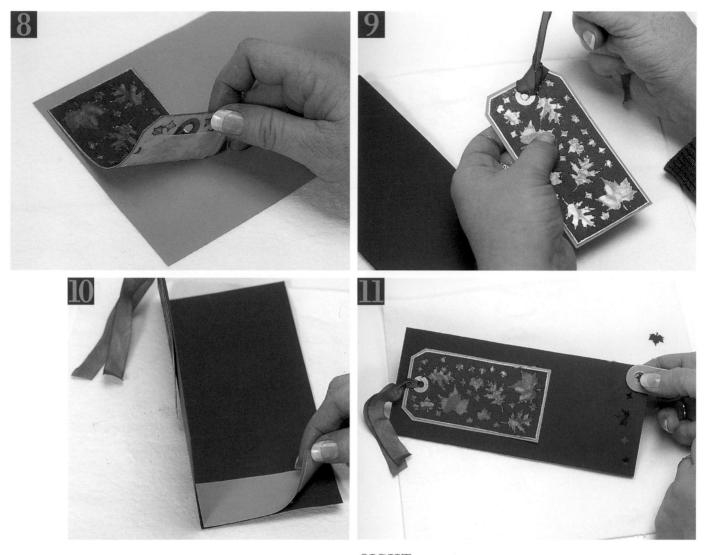

eight: Layer the tag on a contrasting piece of paper; trim to leave a ¼" (6mm) edge.

nine: Add a coordinating ribbon and layer the tag element on a tall card.

ten: For an extra touch, add a strip of the contrasting paper to the inside bottom of the card.

eleven: Finish by punching a few tiny leaves along the front bottom edge of the card.

corset card

These corset (or banded) cards are great fun to unwrap when you use

fancy ribbons, wild fibers and charms. Punches are again the key to

achieving a lacy look. The more you punch, the

fancier it looks!

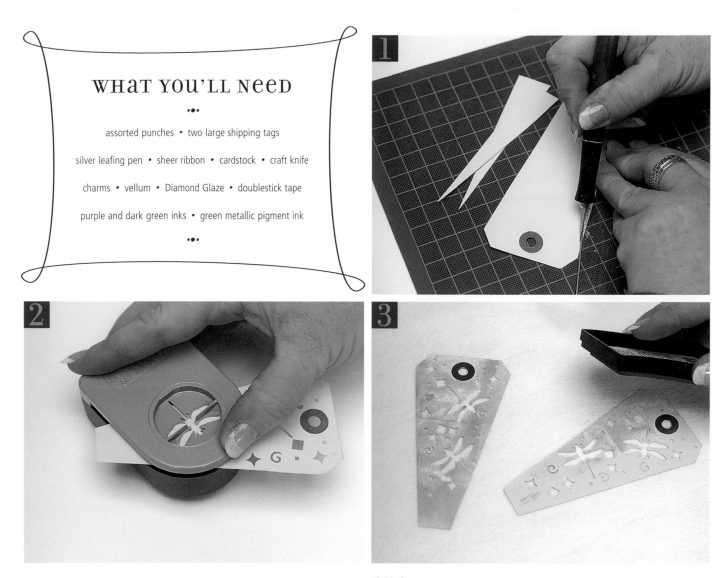

WHAT YOU'LL NEED
•••

assorted punches • two large shipping tags

silver leafing pen • sheer ribbon • cardstock • craft knife

charms • vellum • Diamond Glaze • doublestick tape

purple and dark green inks • green metallic pigment ink

•••

one: Cut two large shipping tags into a triangular shape.

Two: Punch out a variety of shapes, creating a lacy-type effect on the tags.

THree: Rub green metallic pigment ink over the tags.

⑽ TIP ⑽

Punch the larger shapes first, then fill in with punches of

decreasing size.

four: With a silver leafing pen, cover the reinforcements and edges. Also add a few drips, streaks and drops.

five: For the underpinning of this corset I stamped a piece of coordinating vellum with purple and dark green inks. Use a few drops of Diamond Glaze to adhere the tags to the vellum.

six: Trim away the extra vellum.

seven: Mark the tags where they will fold around the card, and score the vellum side of the tags so they will fold easily.

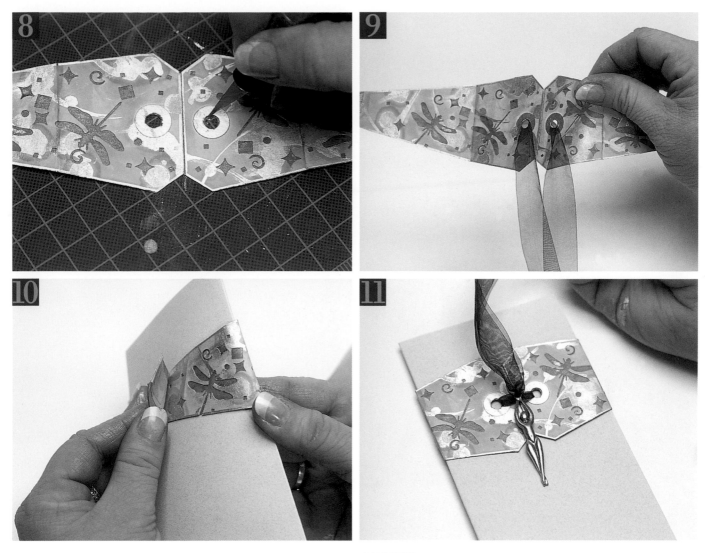

TIP

I have scored the tags with the back side of my craft knife. This creates a very sharp crease.

TIP

A corset band can be made to open in the front by cutting the front seam open with a craft knife.

eIGHT: Trim out the holes of the tags.

nIne: Thread a piece of sheer ribbon through the holes.

Ten: Wrap the corset around the card and secure with doublestick tape.

eLeven: Add a large silver charm or bead. The card should be opened by sliding the whole corset up over the top of the card.

chapter seven

I cannot resist cool fibers, ribbons or thread, and since I do not

sew, it is hard to justify buying them. Then I tried this technique

with the same fabric bond we have used in a previous chapter—what

fun! These fiber cards are a joy to make, and they're so simple and

quick! I try to choose natural fibers when possible. Nylon is not a

good thing near a hot iron!

FIBERS

circle
FIBER *card*

Connect your favorite fibers, threads and ribbons with fabric bond. Any

basic shape will work as a base. Here I have used a circle—I have lots of

leftover circles! Experiment—don't forget the charms.

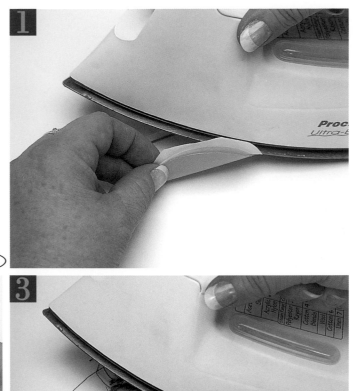

WHAT YOU'LL NEED

•••

assorted natural fibers • charms • handmade paper

fabric bond • colored cardstock

doublestick tape • chipboard *(cardboard)*

iron • scissors • needle and thread

•••

ONE: Using a round piece of cardstock or chipboard as a base, iron on a piece of bonding material. Remove the backing.

TWO: Cut the fibers into smaller bits of varying lengths; lay an assortment on the bonded side of the cardstock.

THREE: Press with a hot iron. Check the fabric bond package direction for the right temperature.

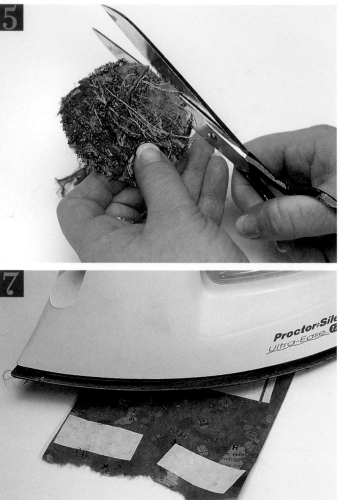

((((TIP))))

You will find the fibers may not cover your cardstock complete-
ly, so add small pieces of the bond to cover those areas. Then
repeat the process.

((((TIP))))

Instead of trimming the fibers to the exact size of the cardstock,
allow a bit of overhang for a rag rug appearance.

FOUr: Turn the piece over and then iron
the cardstock side.

FIVe: Leave a little edge when trimming. Simply even up the fibers. The edge of
the cardstock should not be showing.

SIX: The background layer on this card
uses a coordinating handmade paper. Tear
some of the edges to correspond with the
ragged fiber element.

seven: Add a few pieces of the bonding to the back.

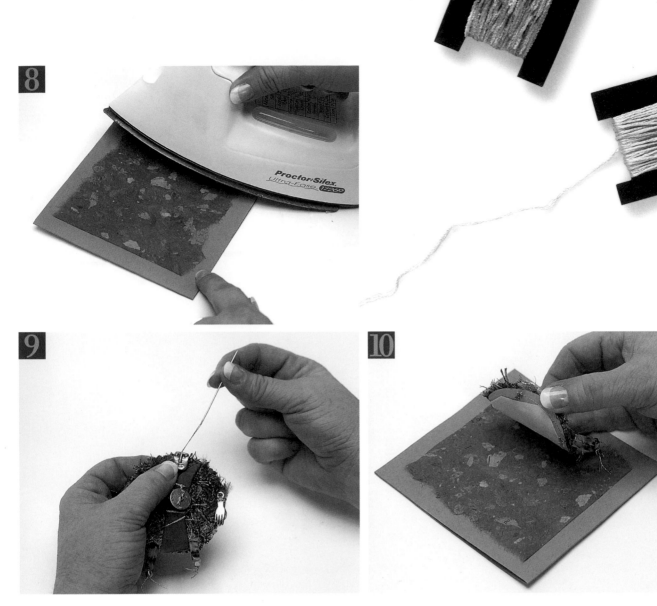

8

9

10

eight: Iron directly onto a piece of cardstock.

nine: Sew on head, hands and feet charms for the character.

ten: Adhere the fiber element to the card with doublestick tape.

((∞ TIP ∞))

The charms do not have to be in the shapes of hands and feet. You can use charms that represent those features. Small bells or beads can be substituted.

((∞ TIP ∞))

This card makes an excellent card/gift. Instead of permanently fixing the fiber element to the card, add a pin back or a cord for a necklace. When creating jewelry, I recommend using colored mat board as the base.

FIBER
KEY *card*

Start this project by cutting a rectangle of cardstock or chipboard and a

piece of bonding material 3" x 4" (8cm x 10cm). Place the bonding piece

on the front of the cardstock. Iron the two pieces together. When cool,

remove the backing from the bond.

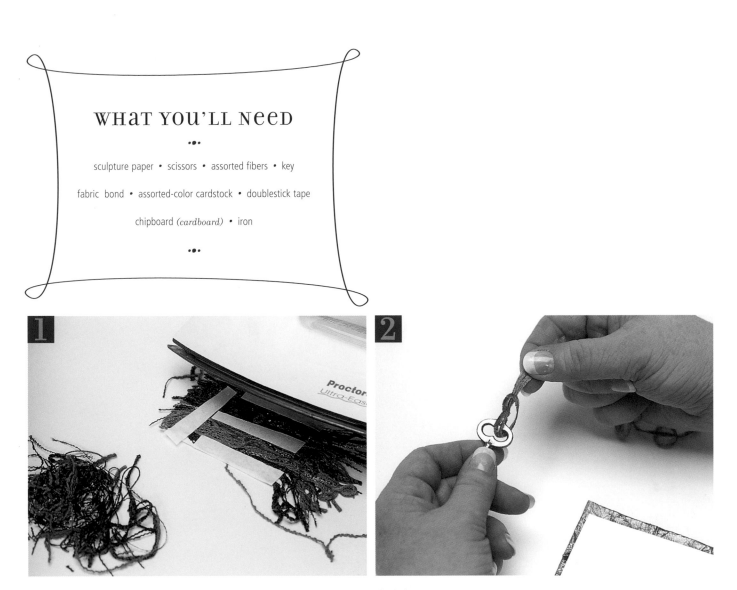

WHAT YOU'LL NEED

...

sculpture paper • scissors • assorted fibers • key

fabric bond • assorted-color cardstock • doublestick tape

chipboard *(cardboard)* • iron

...

one: Cut an array of beautifully colored threads, narrow silk ribbons and fancy yarns to lay on the cardstock. Leave at least ⅛" (3mm) overhang on all sides. Cover the piece generously. Add more bonding pieces as needed over the fibers, then iron over the entire piece.

TWO: Tie a piece of chenille or ribbon to an old key or charm.

TIP

Metallic threads add dramatic flair to natural fibers and silk ribbons.

THree: Tie the key to the fiber piece, and wrap extra chenille around the base.

Four: A piece of sculpture paper is a great background to this fiber art. Fold the edges back to the desired size.

TIP

Try old skate, luggage or drum keys instead of door keys. Seek out antique stores, army surplus stores and flea markets for old, flat metal objects that can be used on greeting cards.

TIP

Try not to trim the fibers too evenly—retain the ragged appearance.

FIVE: Add a light-colored layer of cardstock.

SIX: Trim away the excess fibers.

seven: Add doublestick tape to the back of the fiber piece. Layer onto the card.

FANCY

chapter eight

I am always on the look out for unusual materials to use on my

latest greetings. I love experimenting with new looks and little sur-

prises. Since most cards are sent in simple envelopes, the size of an

embellishment is very important. Look for items no thicker than $\frac{1}{4}$".

Otherwise you will need a box for mailing.

COOL
TRINKETS

cute
crystal *card*

Watch crystals are not always easy to find but are well worth the hunt.

You'll find specific resources in the back of the book. I am using watch

crystals that are new and plastic. Check out

antique stores or Internet auctions for old crystals

or timepiece dealers for new glass ones.

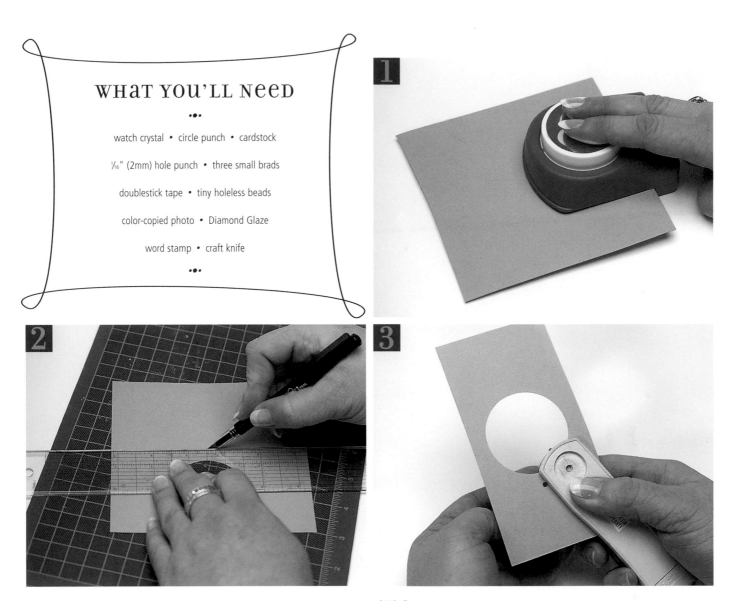

WHAT YOU'LL NEED

•••

watch crystal • circle punch • cardstock

1/16" (2mm) hole punch • three small brads

doublestick tape • tiny holeless beads

color-copied photo • Diamond Glaze

word stamp • craft knife

•••

ONE: Punch a circle from a piece of card-stock. Push the punch in as far as possible.

TWO: Trim away the excess of the cardstock leaving ½" (1cm) on either side.

THREE: Punch three small circles (1/16" [2mm]) along the top of the large circle.

TIP

Try punching wax paper to help paper punches work more smoothly.

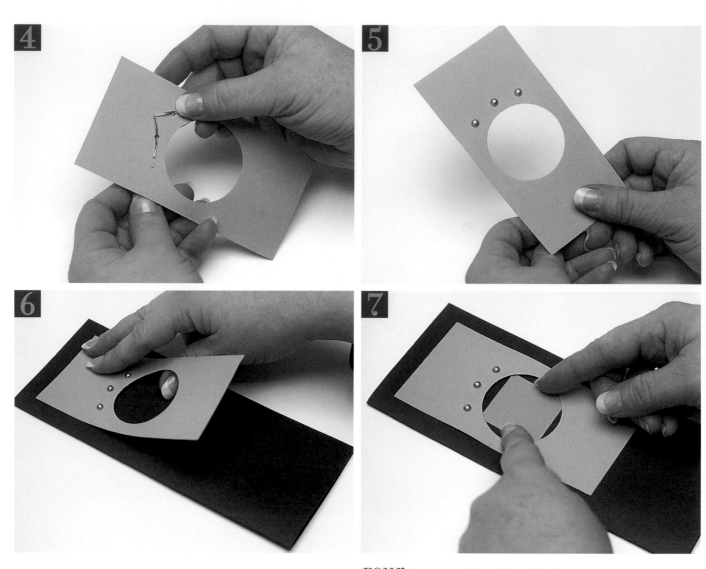

FOUR: Insert small brads into the tiny circles. Bend the prongs back tightly.

FIVE: Check the front of the frame to be certain the prongs are hidden.

SIX: Using doublestick tape at the top and bottom of the frame only, apply the piece to the front of a tall card.

seven: For added contrast, punch a 1" (3cm) square from pale green card-stock. Apply doublestick tape to the back, then insert the square into the circle frame. Set aside.

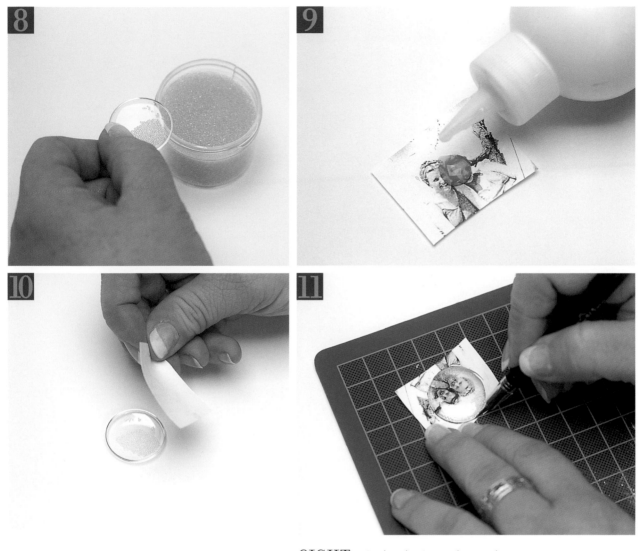

TIP

While the Diamond Glaze is damp, pull the copy gently to flatten the surface before applying it to the rim of the crystal.

EIGHT: Dip the plastic watch crystal into the tiny holeless beads. Leave the crystal open side up on the table while you prepare the paper backing.

nine: Use a color copy of an old photo as the backing to the crystal. Apply a small amount of Diamond Glaze evenly over the surface of the copy.

TEN: Allow the copy to dry for 30 seconds, then apply carefully to the rim of the crystal. Allow this piece to dry in this position for 20 minutes.

eLeven: Trim the excess paper from the watch crystal edge.

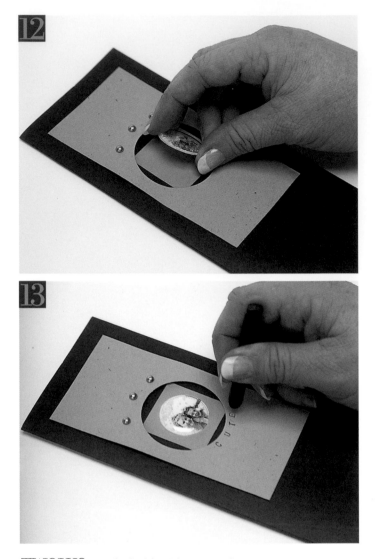

TWELVE: Apply doublestick tape to the back of the finished crystal. Attach the crystal to the card.

THIRTEEN: Using black dye ink and a small alphabet stamp, stamp a word along the bottom of the circle frame.

fancy
aunt *card*

This is one of my favorite photos of my Aunt Caroline. I have color-copied

it many times to use on cards, journals, boxes and jewelry. I think she

would have liked it too since she looks so svelte! The mica tiles add to the

heirloom look of the photo, and this

technique is a great way to use the

smaller tile pieces.

FANCY

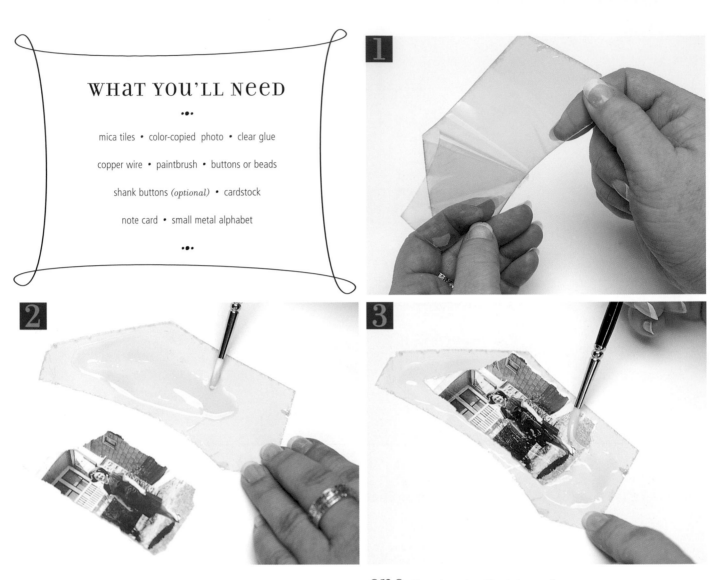

WHAT YOU'LL NEED

•◦•

mica tiles • color-copied photo • clear glue

copper wire • paintbrush • buttons or beads

shank buttons *(optional)* • cardstock

note card • small metal alphabet

•◦•

one: Tear the mica tiles into smaller, thinner pieces.

TWO: Tear away the edges of the photo-copy. Apply a thin layer of clear glue with a paintbrush to the surface of the tile.

THREE: Layer the copy on the tile, then cover the photo with clear glue.

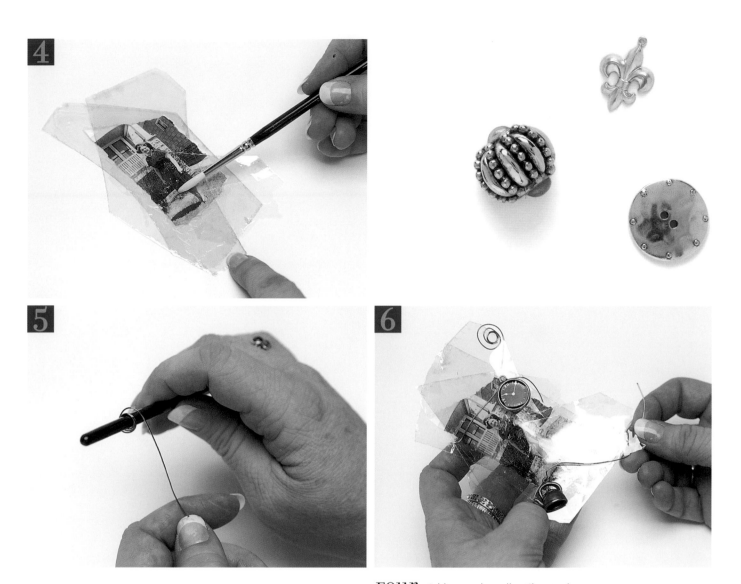

FOUR: Add several smaller tiles to the top of the copy.

FIVE: Twist copper wire around the handle of a paintbrush to create even swirls. Add buttons or beads on the wire.

SIX: Arrange the wire around the mica tile pieces, leaving swirled ends on the front of the piece.

((((TIP))))

Shank buttons can be difficult to use on some projects, but for this project they can be the perfect embellishment, especially if they are from the same era as the photo. Military shanks would be great on old army or navy photos!

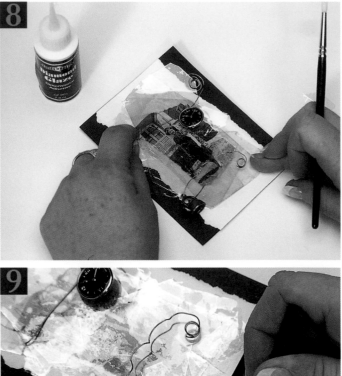

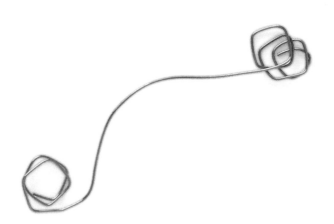

seven: Apply a thin layer of clear glue to a note card; add a torn piece of contrasting cardstock to the front.

eight: Using more clear glue, layer the tile piece to the front of the card.

nine: Stamp a word on a tiny flag of paper with a small metal alphabet. Attach it by curling it around a wire.

rusty
DRAGONFLY *card*

There are many interesting metal pieces available at craft, stamp and

paper arts stores. These particular pieces come in many shapes and sizes

and are rusted and ready to go!

WHAT YOU'LL NEED

••

metal dragonfly • white iridescent ink pad • beads

copper wire • small hammer • metal alphabet

clear glue • blue cardstock • 1" (3cm) square punch

swirl punch • decorative papers • Asian stamp

blue dye ink • thin copper sheet

••

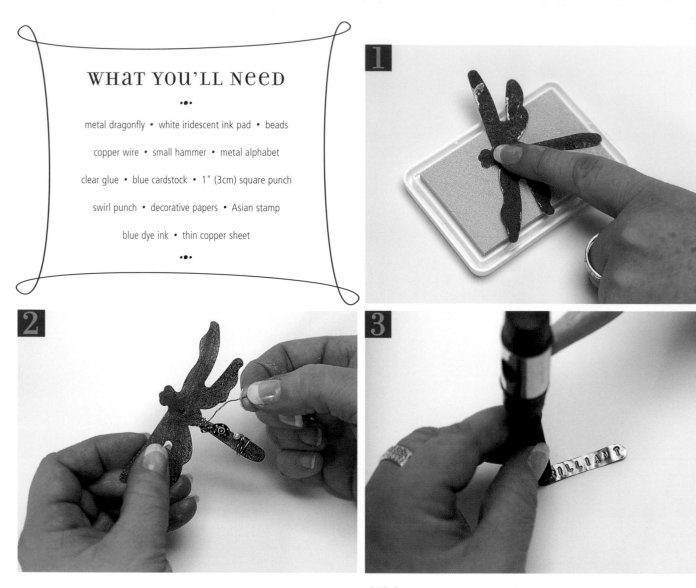

ONE: To soften the color of the metal, apply white iridescent ink directly on the dragonfly. Let dry.

TWO: Decorate the front of the dragonfly with copper wire strung with beads.

THREE: Using a metal alphabet and a small hammer, stamp a word into a thin copper sheet.

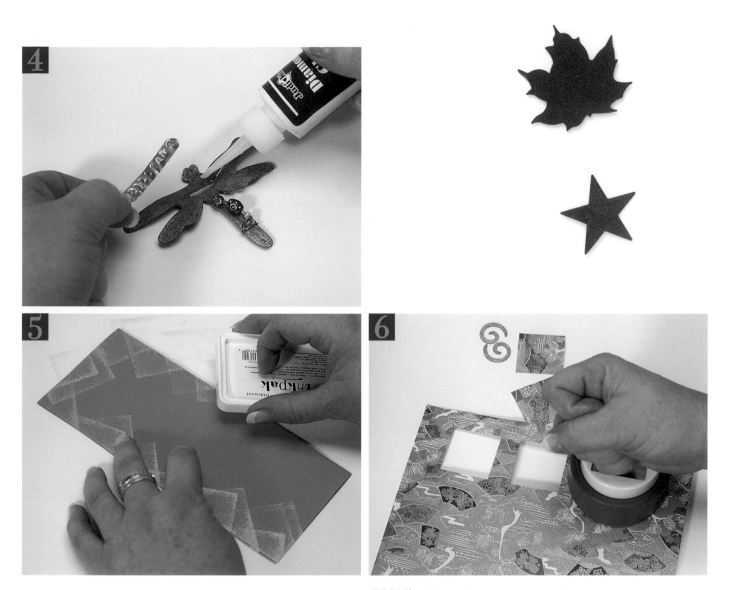

(oo) TIP (oo)

If you like a softer appearance, use a sea sponge to apply the

iridescent ink to the edge of the card.

FOUR: Adhere the copper piece to the dragonfly with a drop or two of clear glue.

FIVE: Lightly dab the same iridescent white ink pad used on the dragonfly to the edge of a tall blue card.

SIX: Punch three 1" (3cm) squares and several swirls out of a decorative printed paper.

seven: Adhere the printed papers as shown directly to the tall card.

eight: Stamp an Asian image along the edge of the cardstock in a medium blue dye ink.

nine: Spread clear glue along the back of the dragonfly, then apply to the front of the card.

framed
GaL *card*

By using foil tape from the local stained glass supplier or stamp store,

you can create a mini-framed photo on the front of your next card. These

little frames make a great decorative

element. Also, you can simply add a pin

to the back of such three-dimensional

items for a neat gift.

WHaT YOU'LL NeeD

···

white gesso • tissue paper • aluminum foil

Diamond Glaze • PearlEx • pink iridescent ink

rubber brush • copy of photo • eyelets • eyelet tool

1" x 1" (3cm x 3cm) piece of clear glass

craft knife • cardstock • small hammer

½" (1.3cm) copper foil tape • doublestick tape

···

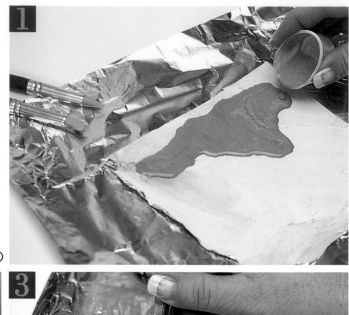

one: Create a piece of sculpture paper (see Chapter Two) by applying white gesso over a piece of tissue paper on aluminum foil. Allow the paper to dry thoroughly, then apply a layer of Diamond Glaze mixed with green PearlEx.

TWO: While the mixture is wet, use a rubber brush to create a pattern in the wet surface. Let dry.

THREE: Dip the rubber brush into pink iridescent ink.

···
108

FOUR: Paint pink iridescent ink into the pattern.

FIVE: Place the piece of glass over the photocopy.

SIX: Crop the photocopy to the size of the glass.

SEVEN: Foil tape is exceptionally sticky, so cut several 1" (3cm) pieces of foil tape before you begin. Apply the foil, leaving an even, straight edge along the photocopy. Press firmly. Trim the foil as each side is applied.

((((TIP))))

Most good hardware stores will cut pieces of glass for you.

EIGHT: With a craft knife, cut holes in the card for the eyelets.

NINE: Insert the eyelets through the sculpture paper and cardstock.

TEN: Use a hammer and setting tool to set the eyelets on the back side of the card.

ELEVEN: Adhere the photo to the card with doublestick tape.

Gallery *of ideas*

✳ A gessoed paper table napkin decorated with paint and stamps makes a unique thank you card.

✳ Use a favorite old family photo in a simple mica tile card.

❊ Use quilt batting under sculpture paper for added height. Fibers, a fancy shank button and a bit of velvet complete the look.

❊ Rich autumn colors add elegance to a plain shipping tag.

✳ Here's a great Mother's Day card perfect for copies of those old photo booth pictures.

✳ Carved shell charms or buttons give an ethnic look to fancy fibers.

✳ Punched symmetrical patterns make an interesting corset card.

✳ Cool beads and wire are easy trinkets to add to graphically simple cards.

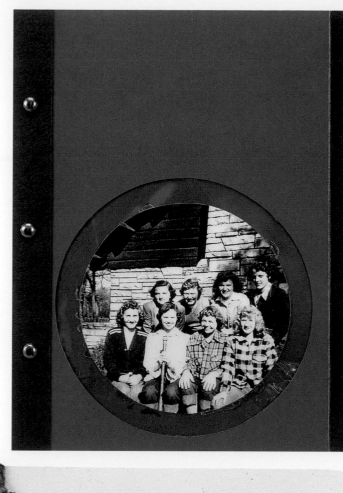

❋ Adding basic elements like brads can create an heirloom quality to a quick mica tile card.

❋ Chenille fibers embedded into the fabric bond in this artsy piece add soft texture to a harsh modern feel.

✷ Shank buttons add an almost military feel to this card, making it the perfect style for Father's Day or dad's birthday.

✷ This wild fiber card, bound with fabric bond to a mica tile, is a great way to announce a party.

❋ High contrast colors work well on unpatterned cardstock.

❋ Glass pebbles surrounded by sculpture paper add depth to tiny photos.

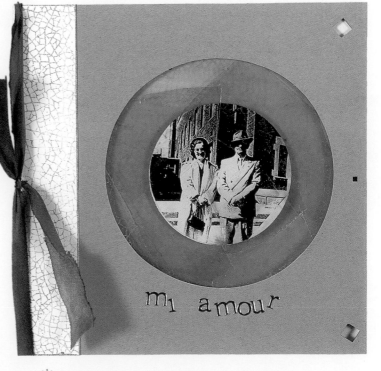

❋ A patterned border and sticker letters can be a fun addition to a modest card, creating a more personal statement for the recipient.

☀ This fancy paper was made from paper towels straight from the kitchen. Pearlized and metallic paints give an elegant feel to this humble paper.

☀ Although trimming fibers closely creates a more uniform element, always leave a few loose threads for interest. Sew larger charms down the center for balance.

✳ Adding smaller tags as embellishments creates the feeling of a gift. A small piece of silk ribbon adds easy elegance.

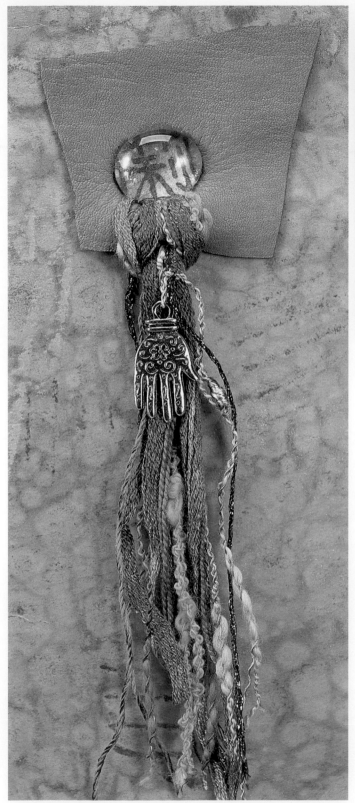

✳ Consider using an old belt or purse leathers to get great textures and colors.

✳ Pull out the colored pencils and add interest to a rubber stamped tag.

☀ Triptychs can be personalized for any occasion with photos, postage stamps and mementos like ticket stubs, tokens or receipts. A combination of ribbons, tassels and stickers can quickly tie a look together.

☀ Pearl florist pins are perfect posts for flags and ribbons. I like to use punches to create see-through areas. Flat game pieces like dominoes or cards are another nice embellishment for triptychs.

Using crayons and punches on the outside of this triptych added texture to a flat plain paper—and provides a nice contrast to the gorgeous marbled paper hidden within. A vellum moon in the center cutout is a fun touch.

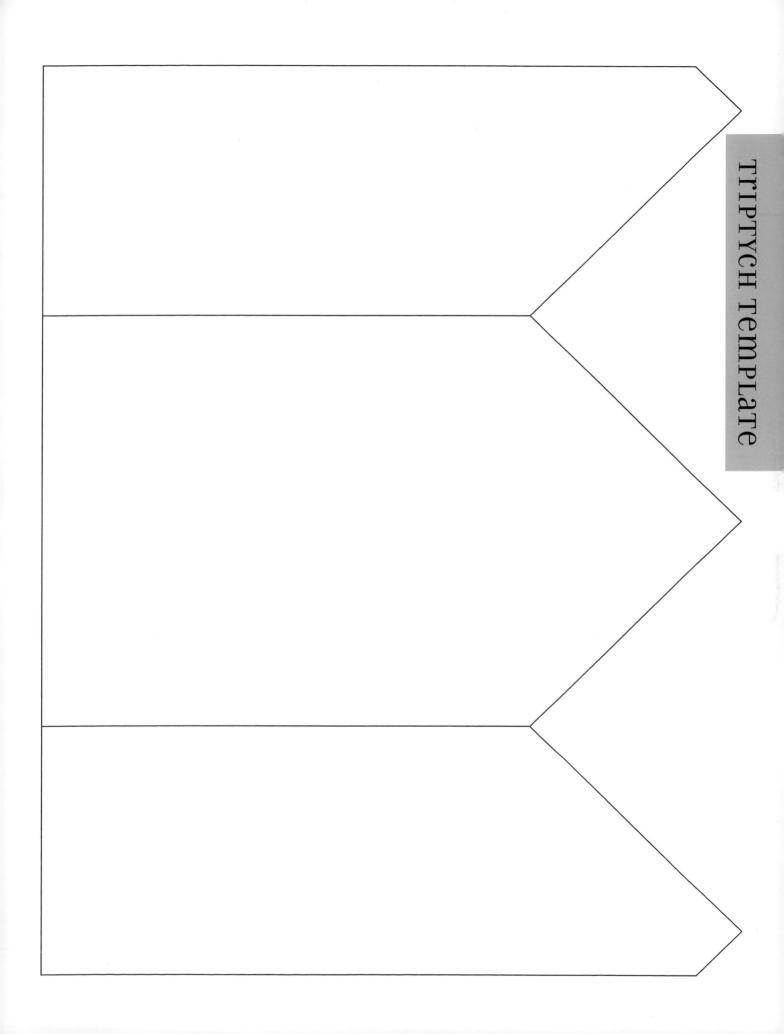

TRIPTYCH TEMPLATE

resources

✳ STAMP, PAPER AND INK COMPANIES

American Art Stamp
3892 Del Amo Blvd
Suite 701
Torrance, CA 90503
(310) 371-6593
www.americanartstamp.com
✳ stamps and supplies

Art Gone Wild
3110 Payne Ave.
Cleveland, OH 44114
(800) 945-3950
Fax: (888) 401-2979
E-mail: artgwild@aol.com
✳ stamps and supplies

A Stamp in the Hand
20630 S. Leapwood Ave. Suite B
Carson, CA 90746
(310) 329-8555
www.astampinthehand.com
✳ stamps

Claudia Rose
15 Baumgarten Road
Saugerties, NY 12477
(914) 679-9235
✳ stamps

Coffee Break Designs
P.O. Box 34281
Indianapolis, IN 46234
E-mail: coffeebreakdesign@ameritech.net
✳ eyelets, watch crystals, brads

ColorBox / Clearsnap / Ancient Page
Box 98
Anacortes, WA 98221
(360) 293-6634
www.clearsnap.com
✳ stamp pads

Craft Connection / Great American Stamp Store
1015 Post Road E.
Westport, CT 06880
(203) 221-1229
✳ stamp supplies, punches

Craft World (head office)
No. 8 North St., Guildford
Surrey GU1 4AF
England
Tel: 07000 757070
✳ retail craft stores

The Creative Block / Stamper's Anonymous
20613 Center Ridge Road
Rocky River, OH 44116
(440) 333-7941
✳ stamps and supplies

Draggin' Ink
P.O. Box 24135
Santa Barbara, CA 93121
(805) 966-5297
✳ templates and supplies

February Paper
P.O. Box 4297
Olympia, WA 98501
(360) 330-6831
✳ fibers and paper

Great American Stamp Store
1015 Post Road East
Westport, CT 06880
(203) 221-1229
✳ assorted punches and supplies

Hobby Crafts (head office)
River Court, Southern Sector
Bournemouth Int'l Airport
Christ Church
Dorset BH23 6SE
England
Tel: 0800 272387
✳ retail craft stores

Hot Potatoes
2805 Columbine Place
Nashville, TN 37204
(615) 269-8002
Fax: (615) 269-8004
www.hotpotatoes.com
✳ stamps and fabric kits

Jacquard Products
Rupert, Gibbon and Spiders, Inc.
P.O. Box 425
Healdsburg, GA 95448
(800) 442-0455
www.jacquardproducts.com
✳ PearlEx, fabric paints, supplies

JudiKins
17803 S. Harvard Boulevard
Gardena, CA 90248
(310) 515-1115
www.judikins.com
✳ Diamond Glaze, stamps, supplies

Krylon Products
101 Prospect Ave., NW
Cleveland, OH 44115
(800) 797-3332
✳ Krylon leafing pens

Lighthouse Memories
(909) 879-0218
www.lighthousememories.com
✳ circle cutters

Magenta
351 Blain
Mont-Saint Hilaire
Quebec, Canada J3H3B4
(514) 446-5253
Fax: (514) 464-6353
www.magentarubberstamps.com
✳ stamps, supplies, paper

McGill
(800) 982-9884
www.mcgillinc.com
✳ punches, scissors

Marvy-Uchida
3535 Del Amo Blvd.
Torrance, CA 90503
(800) 541-5877
Fax: (800) 229-7017
www.uchida.com
✳ dye inks and supplies

Meer Image
P.O. Box 12
Arcata, CA 95518
www.meerimage.com
✳ stamps

Pam Bakke Paste Papers
303 Highland Drive
Bellingham, WA 98225
(360) 738-4830
✳ handmade papers

Paper Parachute
P.O. Box 91385
Portland, OR 97291-0385
✳ stamps and supplies

paula best Rubberstamps
445 La Coches Court
Morgan Hill, CA 95037
(408) 778-1018
www.paulabest.com
✳ stamps and silver charms

On the Surface
P.O. Box 8026
Wilmette, IL 60091
✳ fibers and beads

Postmodern Design
P.O. Box 720416
Norman, OK 73070
✳ stamps and supplies

Postscript Studio / Carmen's Veranda
P.O. Box 1539
Placentia, CA 92871
(888) 227-6367
www.postscriptstudio.com
✳ stamps and supplies

Rubber Monger
P.O. Box 1777
Snowflake, AZ 85937
Fax: (888) 9MONGER
✳ stamps

Rubbermoon
P.O. Box 3258
Hayden Lake, ID 83835
(208) 772-9772
www.rubbermoon.com
✳ stamps

Ruby Red Rubber
P.O. Box 2076
Yorba Linda, CA 92885
(714) 970-7584
✳ stamps

Scattered Pictures
(503) 252-1888
✳ scrapbooks supplies and stickers

Skycraft Designs / Papers
26395 S. Morgan Road
Estacada, OR 97023
(503) 630-7173
✳ handmade papers, pastels, supplies

Speedball
P.O. Box 5157
2226 Speedball Rd.
Statesville, NC 28687
(704) 838-1475
Fax: (704) 838-1472
www.speedballart.com
✳ C-thru ruler and supplies

Stamp Addicts
Park Lane Lodge, Park Lane
Gamlingay
Bedfordshire SG19 3PD
England
Phone/fax: 01767 650329
E-mail: info@stampaddicts.co.uk
www.stampaddicts.com
✳ stamps and stamp supplies

Stamp Camp
P.O. Box 222091
Dallas, TX 75222
(214) 830-0020
✳ stamps

Stamp Your Heart Out
141-C Harvard
Claremont, CA
(909) 621-4363
www.stampyourheart.com
✳ Japanese screw punch, stamps, supplies

Stamp Your Art Out
9685 Kenwood Rd
Cincinnati, OH 45242
www.stampawayusa.com
✳ templates, supplies, stamps

Stampa Rosa Inc.
2322 Midway Dr.
Santa Rosa, CA 95405
(707) 527-8267
www.stamparosa.com
✳ stamps and supplies

Toybox Rubber Stamps
P.O. Box 1487
Healdsburg, CA 95448
(707) 431-1400
Fax: (707) 431-2048
✳ stamps and supplies

Twenty Two
6167 N. Broadway #322
Chicago, IL 60660
✳ stamps

USArtquest
7800 Ann Arbor Road
Grass Lake, MI 49240
(517) 522-6225
www.usartquest.com
✳ mica tiles and supplies

Viva Las Vegastamps
1008 East Sahara Avenue
Las Vegas, NV 89104
(702) 836-9118
www.stampo.com
✳ stamps and supplies

Wilde Ideas
(800) 558-8680
www.wilde-ideas.com
✳ Xyron machines

Zettiology / The Studio Zine
P.O. Box 5681
Bellevue, WA 98006
www.zettiology.com
✳ stamps and magazine

✳ PUBLICATIONS

The Rubberstamper
225 Gordons Corner Road
P.O. Box 420
Manalapan, NJ 07726-0420
(800) 969-7176
www.therubberstamper.com

Rubberstampmadness
408 SW Monroe #210
Corvallis, OR 97330
(541) 752-0075
www.rsmadness.com

Stamper's Sampler & Somerset Studio
22992 Millcreek, Suite B
Laguna Hills, CA
(714) 380-7318
www.somersetstudio.com

Vamp Stamp News
P. O. Box 386
Hanover, MD 21076-0386
Fax: (410) 760-1495
vampstamp@prodigy.net

✳ MY FAVORITE PRODUCTS

Coffee Break Designs
✳ mini beads, eyelets, watch crystals, tiny brads
ColorBox
✳ pigment inks, Ancient Page inks
Draggin' Ink
✳ embossing powders, templates
February Papers
✳ decorative threads and yarns
Great American Stamp Store
✳ assorted punches
Judikins
✳ acetate, laminating sheets, Diamond Glaze, picture pebbles, ROXS
Jacquard Products
✳ PearlEx
Krylon
✳ gold, silver and copper leafing pens
Lighthouse Memories
✳ circle cutter

Lyra
✳ watercolor crayons, pastel chalks
Marvy
✳ dye inks
McGill
✳ punches
On the Surface
✳ fibers
Pam Bakke Paste Papers
✳ specialty papers
Scattered Pictures
✳ assorted punches, scrapbooking stickers
Skycraft Designs
✳ specialty papers
Speedball
✳ C-thru ruler
Stamp Your Heart Out
✳ Japanese screw punch
USArtquest
✳ PearlEx, mica tiles
Wilde Ideas
✳ Xyron supplies

Stamps Used in this Book:
page 18, Paper Parachute. page 20, Judikins. page 21, Rubbermoon. page 30, Ruby Red Rubber. page 35, Stamp Camp. page 39, Judikins. page 43, Rubbermoon. page 44, Rubbermoon. page 46, Postscript Studio. page 48, Postscript Studio. page 49, Judikins. page 52, Postscript Studio. page 57, Rubbermoon. page 64, Twenty Two. page 67, River City. page 84, River City. page 94, Zettiology. page 99, Zettiology. page 106, Judikins. page 111, Postscript Studio. page 117, Judikins. page 119, Rubbermoon, Stamper's Anonymous, Judikins. page 120, Judikins. page 121, Judikins. page 122, paula best.

MaryJo is available to answer questions about all her books through her website:

✳ **www.maryjomcgraw.com** ✳

INDEX